James Gale Inglis

Northern Michigan. Handbook for Travelers

Including the Northern Part of Lower Michigan, Mackinac Islan....

James Gale Inglis

Northern Michigan. Handbook for Travelers
Including the Northern Part of Lower Michigan, Mackinac Islan....

ISBN/EAN: 9783337209810

Printed in Europe, USA, Canada, Australia, Japan

Cover: Foto ©Andreas Hilbeck / pixelio.de

More available books at **www.hansebooks.com**

NORTHERN MICHIGAN.

Handbook for Travelers,

INCLUDING THE

Northern Part of Lower Michigan,

Mackinac Island,

AND THE

Sault Ste. Marie River,

With Maps and Illustrations.

By JAMES GALE INGLIS

GEO. E. SPRANG, Publisher, Petoskey, Mich.

1898.

ALL RIGHTS RESERVED

Table of Contents.

❖❖❖

Introduction.

I. Northern Michigan—Geographical Situation.
II. The Great Lakes—General Information.
III. The Peninsulas of Michigan—Geological History.
IV. The Topography of Michigan.
V. Transportation Facilities.
VI. Climate and Clothing
VII. Baggage, Hotel Life, Fees, Etc.
VIII. Amusements—Tennis, Golf, etc.; Bathing, Boating, Driving, Bicycling.
IX. Camping, Fishing, Hunting, Game Laws.

PART I—Routes to Northern Michigan.

BY RAIL.

I. From Chicago to Grand Rapids:
    a. Via Chicago & West Michigan Railway.
    b. Via Grand Rapids & Indiana Railway (Grand Trunk to Vicksburg).
II. From Detroit to Grand Rapids:
    a. Via Detroit, Grand Rapids & Western Railway.
    b. Via Detroit, Grand Haven & Milwaukee Railway.
III. From Grand Rapids to Traverse City, Petoskey, Mackinaw City.
    a. Via Grand Rapids & Indiana Railway.
    b. Via Chicago & West Michigan Railway.
IV. From Detroit to Bay City, Cheboygan and Mackinaw City, via Michigan Central Railway.

BY STEAMER.

I. From Chicago to Petoskey & Mackinac.
II. From Detroit to Mackinac.

PART II—Grand Traverse Bay.

1. Traverse City and Immediate Environs.
2. From Traverse City to Northport.
    The Leelanaw Peninsula.
3. From Traverse City to Old Mission
    The Old Mission Peninsula.
4. From Traverse City to Charlevoix.
    (1) By Rail.
    (2) Via Elk Rapids and Intermediate Lakes.

PART III—Little Traverse Bay.

1. Charlevoix and Immediate Environs.
2. Excursions from Charlevoix.
    (1) Pine Lake.
    (2) To East Jordan by Carriage Road.
    (3) To Beaver Island.
3. Petoskey and Immediate Environs.
4. Little Traverse Bay from Petoskey to Harbor Springs.
5. Excursion to Cross Village.
6. Excursions from Petoskey.
    (1) To Mackinac Island by rail
        via Mackinaw City.
    (2) The Inland Route.
    (3) Bear Lake.

PART IV—Mackinac Island and Upper Peninsula.

1. Introduction (historical).
2. Mackinac Island.
3. Environs of Mackinac Island.
4. From Mackinac Island to Sault Ste. Marie.

PREFACE.

❦❦❦

THE object of this Handbook for Northern Michigan is to supply the traveler with reliable information concerning the points of interest in the various places visited, the natural features of the country, and the provisions for his entertainment, comfort and transportation. In a word, in every way to aid him in deriving the utmost pleasure and profit from his tour in this beautiful and fascinating region.

This Handbook undertakes to be what the now famous "Baedecker's" are to the countries which they cover. Of course the widely differing conditions require different treatment in detail, but the dignity, accuracy and completeness of the Baedecker guides are the qualities aimed at in the compilation of this book. The whole work is based upon the personal knowledge of the author and publisher, who have long been residents of the region described, and no pains have been spared to make this book as complete and perfect as possible.

There are few regions that offer more fascinating and varied attractions to the intelligent traveler than northern Michigan. To its charm of location, swept by three great inland seas, is added the marvelous health-giving properties of its climate. The scenery is unrivaled in the world, varying from the weird and gorgeous grandeur of Pictured Rocks to the dainty beauty of the Sault Ste. Marie River or the exquisite contour of Little Traverse Bay which rivals, both in situation and color, the famous Bay of Naples.

The native wildness of a great part of this region is an added charm. Its waters teem with fish, its forests with game. Innumerable inland lakes of rarest beauty afford a paradise for those who enjoy "camping out," exploring, and the sports of forest and stream.

In foreign countries whose civilization reaches back into the Past for centuries, the principal points of interest are ancient ruins, great cathedrals, art galleries, museums and historic monuments. While these will not be found here, yet the historic interest of this country is by no means insignificant, for it reaches back to the earliest French and English explorers and includes much that was central of colonial and early American history. The, alas, too rapidly disappearing landmarks of old Indian and early American life add increasing importance to the appreciation and preservation of the priceless fragments which yet remain.

It further remains to be noted that a country which stands first in the production of copper, iron and lime, whose shores are strewn with corals and agates, whose rocks are full of fossils rare and beautiful, must have an interest to the scientific traveler of no small importance. In recent years increasing and remarkably improved facilities for travel have made the charms of this country easily accessible to travelers from all points, so that every year increases by hundreds, if not thousands, the number of those who seek rest and pleasure on its shores.

Progress in this direction has been very marked in recent years. Fine vestibuled trains are run daily by the Grand Rapids & Indiana Railway to Petoskey, Bay View and Mackinaw City, and by the Chicago & West Michigan Railway to Traverse City, Charlevoix, Petoskey and Bay View. Complete suburban service to various resorts and fishing grounds is everywhere provided. The Michigan Central R. R. and the Detroit, Grand Rapids & Western R. R. are through connecting lines with perfect connections with the east, while the Detroit, South Shore & Atlantic R. R. and the Minneapolis, St. Paul and Sault Ste. Marie R. R. continue the service from St. Ignace and the Sault across the upper peninsula to Marquette, Escanaba, Duluth, St. Paul, Minneapolis and the west.

Transportation by water is equally complete. From eastern ports the Northern Transportation Co. have two magnificent steamers, the Northland and the Northwest (see page 51) making through trips from Cleveland, Buffalo and Detroit to Mackinac and Duluth, and the Duluth & Cleveland Steam Navigation Co. continue their justly popular service. While from Chicago we have the old reliable boats of the Seymour line, the Petoskey and Charlevoix, and the palatial express steamer Manitou of the Lake Michigan and Lake Superior line (see page 46).

All these facts combine to make an imperative demand for a carefully prepared Handbook which will indicate, not only the prominent points of interest, but others equally important that might easily escape the transient traveler's notice; which will give brief but accurate description of the points of historic and scientific interest; which will direct the sportsman to the places he most desires to find—in short a guide to every traveler, which will enable him to get quickly and readily from place to place, to enjoy intelligently what he sees, and to inform himself reliably concerning that which he most wishes to know.

The Handbook is divided into four parts beside the Introduction. Part One covers the various routes by which Northern Michigan may be reached and aims to give a rapid but complete sketch of the special items of interest which the traveler will pass en route. The other three divisions are based upon the three geographical districts into which the country described is naturally divided, namely: Part Two, Grand Traverse Bay, including Traverse City with adjacent peninsulas. Part Three, Little Traverse Bay, including Charlevoix, Petoskey, Harbor Springs, the Inland Route and their environs. Part Four, Mackinac Island, including the Cheneaux Islands (the "Snows"), St. Ignace and the Sault Ste. Marie River.

As far as possible the descriptions have been prepared to embrace, in the details of the various routes, every item of interest, historic, scientific, scenic and general. It could hardly be hoped that mistakes do not occur, but the reader is assured that great care has been taken to avoid them. Any suggestions or corrections that may be noted in the actual use of the Handbook will be greatly appreciated by the author. The index in the back of the book will be found of value for ready reference.

While advertisements have been admitted into one edition in order to reduce the cost, scrupulous care has been taken to secure their absolute reliability, and they have been limited to those lines of trade concerning which the traveler most desires to know. In other words, nothing has been admitted merely for the sake of advertising, the needs of the reader being the sincere and single aim of this book. A library edition, without advertisements and bound in cloth, is also published and is commended to those who may find the book worthy of more than passing interest.

The maps and plans have been carefully prepared

and will, it is believed, be ample assistance to the traveler. The illustrations are abundant and chosen with a view to preserve many glimpses of a rapidly-disappearing life, as well as to illustrate the charms and beauties of this enchanted land. Together with the more prominent hotels, a list of private boarding houses is given, where those who prefer quieter living may secure comfortable accommodations at reasonable rates. While in this, as in other items of local information, every pains has been taken to secure accuracy, yet it will be remembered by the reasonable reader that changes are inevitable in all communities, and due allowance will be made.

Grateful appreciation of the assistance so cordially rendered in every community in the preparation of this Handbook, is hereby acknowledged. Special thanks are due to the officials of the Chicago & West Michigan R. R., the Grand Rapids & Indiana R. R., the Arnold Steamboat line, the Lake Michigan and Lake Superior Transportation Co. and the Northern Steamship Co. Also to Mr. Fred. B. Stimpson of Petoskey, Mr. W. O. Brunner of Grand Rapids, Mr. Thomas T. Bates of Traverse City, Mr. W. M. Spice of St. Ignace, for special favors rendered.

The preparation of this Handbook, while an arduous has been a pleasant task. Our sincere wish is that it will be practically useful to the traveling public and add something to the pleasure and profit of a trip through this delightful country.

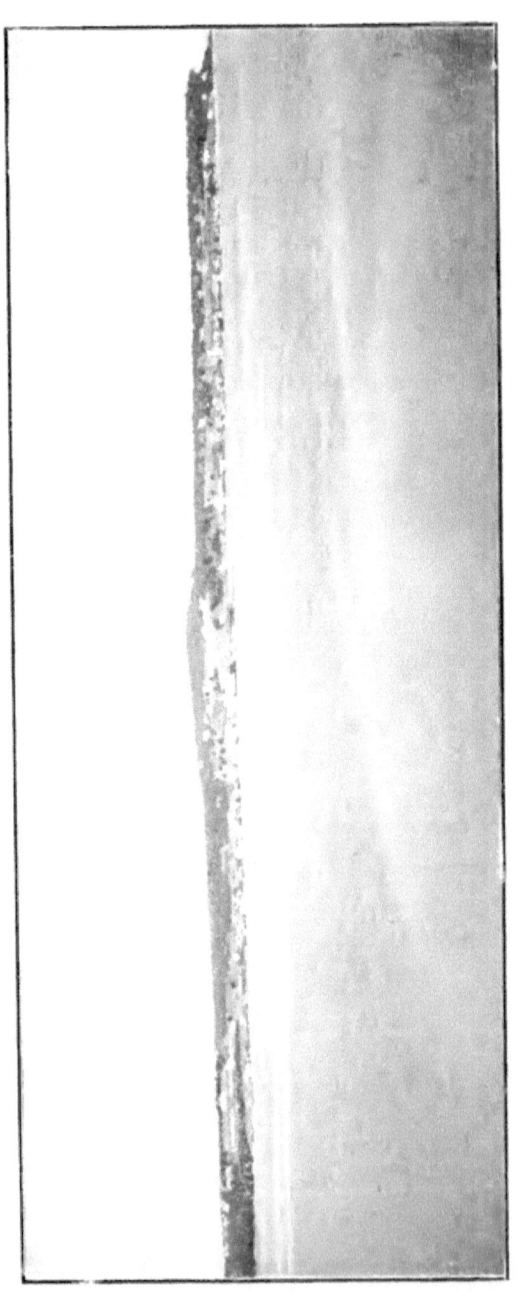

MACKINAC ISLAND.

INTRODUCTION.*

I.

NORTHERN MICHIGAN, Geographical Situation.

THE first impressions of Niagara Falls are those of awe-inspiring grandeur. One wishes to contemplate in silence the sublime spectacle, all other thoughts being overwhelmed by the majesty of that mighty cataract. Gradually, however, details begin to suggest themselves. The dizzy height, the deafening thunder of those falling waters, the wildness of the gorge with its raging torrent, the power displayed. All these and more begin to make distinct impressions on the mind.

Among these details nothing is more impressive than the sense of the immensity of that torrent. The mind tries in vain to estimate in gallons or in tons the quantity of water plunging incessantly over that precipice, and the question at once arises, where does it come from—this unfailing and exhaustless flood?

If, with this thought in mind, the reader will glance at any good map of North America, he will gain a new conception of the significance of Niagara Falls. He will

---

*Several sections of this introduction do not concern the immediate needs of the traveler. They are written for the information of those who desire to know something of the geologic history and the geographical significance of the region they are about to visit, and may be omitted without impairing the usefulness of the rest of the book. Yet it is hoped that most readers will find their perusal a pleasant and profitable employment for quiet moments on steamboat or train when not employed in actual sight-seeing.

find that over its heights sweep the waters of four great inland seas whose floods gather volume in ever increasing ratio from the immense areage of which this system is the watershed.

In the very center of these great waterways lies the region known as Northern Michigan. Its position is strategic and unique. One great peninsula pushes northward between Lakes Michigan and Huron, blunt in form, 300 miles long and 150 miles wide. Another great peninsala pushes eastward, long and narrow in form, between Lakes Michigan and Superior, 300 miles long and about 75 miles wide. At the point where these two peninsulas and three great lakes meet, lies Mackinac Island, the geographical and historic center of this wonderful country.

II.

THE GREAT LAKES, General Information.

The four Great Lakes, Superior, Michigan, Huron and Erie, whose waters pour over Niagara's precipice, embrace a mean shore line of 4,500 miles. They drain and irrigate a country that may be roughly estimated at 400 miles square. In this connection should be noted the remarkable fact that none of these lakes receives the waters of any great river. In fact only a narrow fringe of land separates them from the other great waterways which touch them at every point. Immediately to the northwest begins the Saskatchewan system with its countless lakes and rivers pouring into Hudson's Bay and draining almost the whole Northwest Territory. To the west, and distant scarcely fifty miles, lies the Mississippi, draining even Minnesota, Wisconsin and Illinois, although these states aggregate almost half of the coast area of the great lakes. The rivers of Indiana and Ohio flow southward to swell the Ohio river, itself a chief tributary to the Mississippi. While to the north the great rivers of Canada flow, not into Lake Superior, but into Hudson's Bay. No rivers larger than the St. Joseph in Michigan or the Nipigon in Canada empty into the Great Lakes, but their vast sweep of drainage area contains countless small lakes and numberless little streams whose waters pour into these great inland seas.

Lake Michigan is 320 miles long, 100 miles in width, and has a total area of 22,000 square miles. Lake Huron is 260 miles long, 160 miles in width, with an area of 24,400 square miles. These lakes have an equal elevation, being 581 feet above the sea. Lake Erie lies about 8 feet below, while Lake Superior lies 20 feet above, being 601 feet higher than the Atlantic Ocean. This matchless lake, the largest body of fresh water in the world, is 355 miles long, 160 miles broad and has the immense area of 31,400 square miles. These great fresh water basins, reaching a depth of over 900 feet (the deepest soundings in Lake Superior show 1200 feet) have been literally carved out by various eroding forces in the cycles of geological formation. The immense mass of sedimentary strata thus put in motion by the same forces, was gradually deposited in "drifts" over a large zone of the northern hemisphere. In the arrangement and rearrangement of this drift is found the problem of later geological formations and present surface conditions.

These vast lakes add to their beauty of scenery, exhaustless water supply, immense fisheries and climatic influence, a commercial usefulness as highways of transportation which is beyond computation. They carry perhaps one-half the grain supply of the world. Across them is transported iron, copper, lumber and other products in quantities whose aggregate sum the mind is unable to comprehend. They afford facilities for intercommunication which open doors of easy access to nearly half the continent.

III.

THE PENINSULAS OF MICHIGAN, Geological History.

The two peninsulas of Michigan form unique dividing barriers between three of these great lakes, like mighty wedges driven in between their rolling seas. These "wedges" have been the battlefield of many a geological period, the center of fiercest conflict between Nature's opposing forces. No one, therefore, can intelligently traverse this country, so varied in formation and fascinating in contour, without some knowledge of its geological history; and no account of this region would be complete without some résumé of those primal, crucial, elements of world building whose sublime drama was enacted on these very shores. The writer therefore ventures to narrate, in brief and simple outline, this geologic history including a section on present conditions and resources, which are but the result of formations whose beginnings reach back into the limitless past.

During those awful convulsions of Nature which mark the earliest (Archaean) period of earth formation the Laurentian Hills, which form the north shore of Lake Superior, were thrown up—a part of that great backbone, which, in the form of a wide-angled V, extended east and west from ocean to ocean across what is now the center of North America, and which was all that then existed of this continent. These gaunt and solemn Laurentian Hills have stood unmoved, unchanged, through almost endless cycles of time, silent spectators of the building of a continent. Michigan, with all the eastern states, was then the bed of a great arm of the sea whose flowing tides dashed against these rocks, now a part of the Canadian shores of Lake Superior.

Then followed a period of land making, (1) by subsidence of the shallow sea; (2) by accumulating deposits of sediments; and (3) by internal disturbances and eruptions. To the latter cause is due the great copper and iron mines with the strange "pudding-stone" formation of Keweenaw peninsula in upper Michigan. To the other two causes are due the general conformation of lower Michigan and the great coal and salt measures which lie beneath its present surface. Michigan was the last to reject the ocean, but finally the barrier was built and what was for long ages a great ocean bay now became an immense fresh water marsh, covered with dense vegetation to be converted finally into beds of bituminous coal.

During the long (Mesozoic) period which followed, the gradual process of rock formation was continued. The immense red sandstone quarries near Portage Canal, the lime formations of the Traverse and Mackinaw districts, rich in cretaceous fossils, and that peculiar soft rock out of which the waters carved, in later days, the far-famed Pictured Rocks of Lake Superior—all these belong to this period. While doubtless at this time there was the beginning of some great depression running along the St. Lawrence valley eastward to the sea, afterwards the channel of the St. Lawrence River, yet the mind must continually force itself to realize that during all these ages there were *no great lakes nor any semblance of them,* but only vast stretches of Silurian and other deposits, the slow foundation-building of our present surface superstructure.

It remained for the fourth and last great period (Cenozoic), to complete the formation as we have it now. The mighty glaciers of the ice age found their natural pathway across this region to the sea. They carved out our great fresh water basins like giant chisels, deepening depressions already begun, emphasizing the sharp distinctions between hard and soft stratifications and leaving on either side, in sublime confusion of moraines, those masses of drift deposits out of which the present topography of Michigan has emerged. After the glaciers, followed great flood periods, of which the Indians have legends, whose mighty tides washed shores that are now the tops of precipices, as at Mackinac Island, and formed those sweeping terraces which make the great plateaus of lower Northern Michigan.

A profile of Michigan with elevations will be found on page 25. A study of this profile at this point will greatly assist the reader.

IV.

THE TOPOGRAPHY OF MICHIGAN.

The present topography of Michigan may be summed up in a single paragraph. The great alluvial plain which sweeps northward from Ohio and embraces about two-thirds of lower Michigan, contains those rich clay deposits which give Michigan front rank in agricultural resources, and beneath which lie the gypsum beds of Grand Rapids, the coal measures of Jackson and the salt wells of Saginaw. Further northward a succession of terraces sweeping from east to west (see profile page 25), marks the wash of a greater sea when Lakes Huron and Michigan were one. The plateau which crowns these terraces was then an island, and the immense lime deposits of that Palaeozoic age were laid there either in regular strata of great ledges such as are now quarried at Petoskey, or in permeations through and through the soil forming the chemical basis of nourishment for the dense forests which afterwards covered this region. The coral formations of Traverse, the grotesque forms of cliffs at Mackinac Island and the Pictured Rocks, the silver and lead mines of Algomah near the Sault Ste. Marie River, the iron of Ishpeming and the copper of Calumet, the agates and pudding stone and mass copper of Keweenaw, and silent over all the eternal Laurentian rocks of Lake Superior's northern shore, all these, in their turn, testify to the endless geologic cycles and fierce cataclysmic changes out of which this wondrous country had its birth.

V.

TRANSPORTATION FACILITIES.

On account of its central location, its resources in lumber, ores and other commercial products and its charm as a place of resort, Northern Michigan has been the center of active transportation operations for many years, while recent facilities for travel have been so increased as to secure to the tourist all that could be asked of speed, comfort and convenience. In the height of the summer season, however, all accommodations—whether by rail or boat—are taxed to their utmost limit, and the traveler should not fail to make early choice of route and selection of berth or stateroom. So great a variety of routes are offered, and each includes so many points or beauty and interest, that if possible the trip should be planned so as to come by one route and return by another. The added value and pleasure of the trip will more than repay the extra expense.

Several trunk lines now run through trains to all prominent points in Northern Michigan. Regular fares are computed at three cents a mile in lower Michigan, and four cents a mile in the upper peninsula, but special excursion tickets may be secured to all points at greatly reduced rates (see schedule preceding index). For details of arrival and departure of trains, boats, etc., the traveler is referred to the time-tables and other helpful and attractive folders issued by the various transportation companies. Wood's Railway Guide, published monthly, is reliable and complete.

VI.

CLIMATE AND CLOTHING.

The climate of Northern Michigan is justly famed for its health-giving properties. It is cool and bracing, and while subject to the usual uncertainties of each season, there are general conditions which are practically unvarying. However warm it may be in the daytime it is always cool at night, so that the traveler should invariably be supplied with wraps or light overcoat for evening use, and ample bedding should be provided for sleeping, especially in summer cottages. Although there is a marked difference (from three to six degrees) between the temperature inland and on the coast of the lakes, nevertheless those who are planning to spend their time on inland lakes and away from coast breezes, should not neglect to provide both for cool evenings and sudden changes.

A suit of not too light material, underwear of medium weight and good stout shoes will be found most serviceable for general use.

VII.

BAGGAGE, HOTEL LIFE, FEES, ETC.

Complete arrangements are provided at all central points for the handling of baggage, both at docks, depots and hotels. Those who plan an extended stay in one place, especially if they expect to enter the social life of the more fashionable hotels and resorts, will need the same quantity and variety of clothing as at home. But all others, especially those who are planning short stays in many places with any considerable amount of traveling, will save trouble and expense by taking as little baggage as possible.

Gratuities, fees, tips to waiters, hotel porters, etc., are not expected and should be indulged in only in exceptional cases. Regular charges are made for all services rendered. There is little attempt at extortion and ordinary courtesy will invariably insure the traveler every assistance he can reasonably expect.

VIII.

OUTDOOR AMUSEMENTS.

Summer life in Northern Michigan abounds in opportunities for outdoor amusement. Tennis, golf and kindred recreations are universal. Boating in all forms is, of course, prominent, and good boats, both row and sail, may be rented at reasonable rates. Bathing is a favorite pastime, especially on the inland lakes. In some places suits may be rented, but generally it will be more satisfactory for those who intend to bathe to be provided with their own.

The roads in Northern Michigan are, for the most part, in fairly good condition, and in many places fine. Beautiful drives abound and good liveries are to be found, even in small towns.

To bicyclers we offer the following suggestions. While the roads are not all that could be desired, and in some places are entirely impracticable, still many quite extended tours can be comfortably made through much charming and otherwise not accessible scenery. In places, notably Mackinac Island, the roads are exceptionally good. Those whose pastime is to be largely bicycling will do well to bring their own wheels, but bicycles can be rented in all the larger towns at reasonable rates. Roads available for wheeling will be noted in detail in connection with the town from which they lead.

IX.

CAMPING, FISHING, HUNTING.

The immense virgin forests of Northern Michigan form one of its most attractive features. Nothing can exceed the exquisite sense of rest and delight which these forests bring to those weary and worn with the strain and tumult of life in a great city. No tourist will do justice to himself or his trip in this region without at least a taste of life in the woods and near to

Nature's heart. The great trees, the gentle murmur of the wind, the rich and beautiful carpeting of mosses and wild flowers, the constantly changing vistas and the restful quietness—all these and more combine to make such an experience rich in pleasure and profit, both to mind and body.

The most practicable way to secure such a trip is to seek some one of the modest yet very comfortable little hotels or inns which may be found on many inland lakes. Rates are very reasonable, the traveler is saved much time, expense and annoyance incident to camping out and has most of its advantages and charms. Those who desire the genuine experience, however, will readily find beautiful locations everywhere on which to pitch their tents. Of course camping may be indulged in on almost any scale, but even in its most simple form the traveler is warned that there is but small economy and much hard work and annoyance. The writer is an experienced camper and yields to none in his enthusiasm for this charming recreation, but deems it only his duty to speak from long experience this honest word of warning, emphasized each year by a long list of bitter disappointments experienced by those who inconsiderately rushed into "camping out" excursions. Favorable locations for camping abound everywhere and final selection can be best made by local inquiry. Outfits can be secured at the larger towns, but it would be better to make them up at home and ship direct to nearest points. Large parties are to be avoided, from six to eight being the maximum. Better make two entirely separate though neighboring camps, if a larger number is necessary.

For life in the forest warm underwear and rough old clothes are desirable. Take nothing into camp, especially in the way of clothing, you are not willing to have spoiled or damaged. Waterproofs, rubbers and stout comfortable shoes are indispensable. A pair of slippers for evening use "around camp" will be a great comfort. These suggestions apply equally to camping out or boarding at inns. In June and the first part of July the mosquitoes are a great annoyance, but they begin to disappear about the middle of July. Various applications known as "mosquito dope" are on sale at drug and hardware stores. They are highly effective and should be secured without fail and freely used.

Fishing is the sport royal of Northern Michigan. For years this region has been the paradise for the ardent disciple of Isaac Walton, and while there is little of what may be called "virgin waters" strictly speaking, nevertheless it is certainly true that this region affords as fine sport for the fisherman as is readily accessible from any of our large towns or cities. The very many streams and lakes available will be noted in detail in their proper places.

Guides can be secured at from $1.00 to $1.50 per day and are desirable, especially if the lake is not well understood. It will be found more satisfactory to remain in one place and "learn" the lake or stream than to go from place to place. In the long run better catches will be made and more real sport enjoyed. Such a plan is more economical also, as in a short time the guide may be dispensed with.

Good hunting may also be enjoyed in season. Partridge, rabbit, fox, lynx, deer and bear are killed in large numbers. We append a resume of the game laws of Michigan now in force.

GAME LAWS.

DEER may be killed from the 1st day of November to the 25th day of November, both inclusive, each year, in both peninsulas. Deer must not be killed or captured in the water, or by pit or trap, or by artificial light, or by use of a dog.

Non-residents who engage in hunting or killing deer, shall be required to take out a license in the county where he proposes to hunt during the open season; license fee, $25.

Residents of six months, who wish to hunt deer, shall take out a license from their county clerk, for which license they shall pay a fee of not more than 50 cents, such license to continue in force only for season issued.

Not more than five deer may be killed by one person in any one year, and on any deer or part of deer shipped, shall be a coupon from said license, signed and detached by person to whom license is issued, in presence of shipping agent at point of shipment.

PARTRIDGE (Ruffled Grouse). November 1st to December 15th inclusive. Upper Peninsula, October 1st to January 1st inclusive.

QUAIL. November 1st to December 15th, inclusive.

WOODCOCK. August 15th to December 15th.

DUCK, WATER FOWL, etc. Jacksnipe, red-head, blue-bill, canvas back, widgeon and pin-tail ducks and wild geese may be killed between September 1st and May 1st. Other wild water fowl and snipe between September 1st and January 1st.

SELLING AND SHIPPING GAME. No person shall expose or keep for sale, directly or indirectly, sell or barter, any quail, woodcock or partridge in the State. Game cannot be shipped to points outside of State at any time.

FISH LAWS.

Speckled trout, land locked salmon and grayling, or California trout, may be caught May 1st to September 1st following.

The killing of fish by the use of dynamite or giant powder or any explosive, or the use of Indian cockle or any substance tending to stupefy the fish is unlawful.

It is unlawful to spear any kind of fish, except mullet, grass pike, red sides and suckers, during the months of March, April, May and June in any of the inland waters of the State.

It is unlawful to catch any fish excepting mullet, red sides and suckers at any time in any of the inland waters of the State by the use of any kind of seines or nets.

Bass, trout and grayling must not be caught in any way, at any time, except by hook and line in the inland waters of the State.

It is not lawful to capture or have in possession any brook trout or grayling less than six inches in length.

Streams in which trout and grayling are not native, stocked with such fish, are protected by law three years after planting of such stream.

It is unlawful to catch minnows for other purposes than for bait.

It is unlawful to fish with a net within a radius of one hundred feet from any fish chute or ladder.

It is unlawful to place in any stream, race or lake any kind of weir dam or any device which may obstruct the free passage of fish.

The purchase, sale, carriage or possession of brook trout or grayling during the closed season is forbidden.

The violation of the law is punishable by fine or imprisonment.

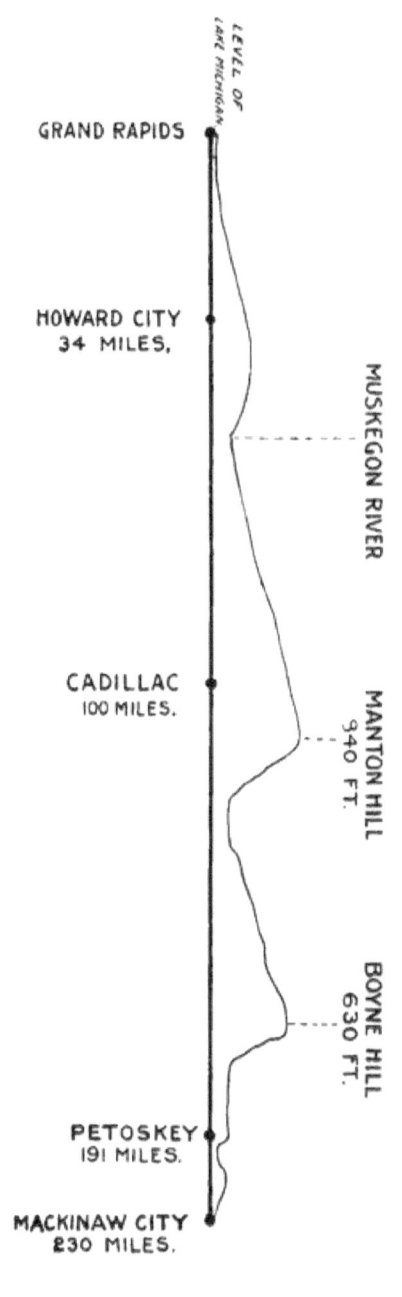

EXPLANATORY NOTES
to Profile on preceding page.

Through the kindness of Mr. Fred B. Stimson of the Grand Rapids & Indiana Railway, we are able to present our readers with a reduced profile of the lower peninsula, setting forth the topography and elevations of Michigan for 230 miles nearly due north and south from Grand Rapids to Mackinaw City, embracing about two-thirds of the lower peninsula. This profile will illustrate the general topographical condition described in Sections III and IV of Introduction.

Beginning with Grand Rapids we note in the smaller plateau the overlapping of that vast alluvial plain which extends northward from Ohio and forms the great agricultural belt of Michigan. From this point a second great plateau rises slowly to the top of Manton Hill, a distance of 110 miles, intersected at 50 miles from Grand Rapids by the Muskegon river. This plateau reveals an intimate relation with the great flood periods when immense deposits of lime were, by later conditions, absorbed into the soil (rather than laid in regular strata) to become the basis of nutriment for the dense and noble forests of pine and hardwood which have covered it. It may be known as the forest-belt of Michigan. It culminates in Manton Hill, 843 feet above the level of Lake Michigan, the highest point of land, from which descent is made to the third plateau.

The third plateau, reaching from Manton Hill to Boyne Hill, represents in its general conditions the same characteristics as that of the second plateau, with this exception, that, being subjected to severer action of the floods, its coast became more indented (e. g. the Grand Traverse Bay), its surface more rugged and uneven. Here, therefore, we find great numbers of inland lakes and small streams, as well as fine forests and abundant limestone formations It culminates in Boyne Hill, 630 feet above the level of Lake Michigan, from which rapid descent is made to the fourth plateau.

The fourth plateau, extending from the foot of Boyne Hill to Mackinaw City, represents that section which was last to reject the water, retaining most of the characteristics of the two previous plateaus, but which, being subjected to even severer action in the rush of waters, shows formations naturally following such conditions, culminating in the lime deposits of Petoskey, the coral laid bare along this coast, and the picturesque waterwear of Mackinac Island, and St. Ignace on the opposite sides of the Straits.

PART I.

ROUTES TO NORTHERN MICHIGAN.

Northern Michigan may be reached both by rail and steamboat from all directions. Three great lines of railway, Chicago & West Michigan, Grand Rapids & Indiana (Pennsylvania Central System) and Michigan Central run through trains to its resorts, and steamboat lines on all the great lakes make regular and frequent trips. A brief description of the various routes is here given, as being of interest and value to the traveler. Chicago, Grand Rapids and Detroit are chosen for the sake of convenience, as the points of departure.

1. From Chicago to Grand Rapids.

a. Via Chicago & West Michigan Railway.

181 miles; time 5¼ hours.

CHICAGO Population 1,500,000, the second city of America and one of the great cities of the world, the center of immense commercial interests and the seat of several universities. Though only sixty years old, and in 1870 almost totally destroyed by fire, this city has had such phenomenal growth as to place it in the front rank and to make it in some respects the foremost city in the world. For details the traveler is referred to special guide books to be had at all news stands and book stores.

The Chicago & West Michigan Railway starts from the Illinois Central depot on the lake front at Park Row.

Wabash Ave. and State St. cable cars run to Park Row and within a short distance of the station. The depot is a magnificent structure, commanding a fine view, and containing one of the finest waiting rooms in the world. It was built in 1893 at a cost of over a million dollars. The Illinois Central, Michigan Central and Chicago & West Michigan Railways center here.

The train passes swiftly over the tracks of the Illinois Central to Kensington (13 miles) close to the shore of Lake Michigan. Four miles out may be seen the "crib" that marks the mouth of the great tunnel which affords the south side water supply of Chicago. On the right we are passing through one of the most beautiful residence portions of the city, stopping for a moment at Hyde Park (5 miles), the location of the Chicago University, and again at Woodlawn Park, 63rd street, (7 miles) the terminus of the south side elevated railway. Between Hyde Park and Woodlawn the train passes close (on the left) to the grounds of the Columbian Exposition, now a public park, part of beautiful Jackson Park. Many of the exposition buildings are still standing, being used for museums and other purposes.

PULLMAN (15 miles)—The extensive works of the Pullman Palace Car Co. are located here in full view of the train on the left. The town of Pullman affords an interesting study as a sociological experiment. A brief visit is well worth time and attention.

HAMMOND (20 miles)—The extensive stock yards and meat packing works of the Hammond Packing Co. may be seen on the left.

The train now speeds over a level and comparatively uninteresting country on the main line of the Michigan Central Railway, leaving Illinois and entering Indiana, whose southwest extremity it traverses for a little time, reaching MICHIGAN CITY (58 miles), an important railway center with a little stream which affords a harbor for small boats. Here we catch a glimpse of Lake Michigan between the great sand-dunes or drift hills of sand. These shifting sand hills in their structure and variations form a most interesting study.

NEW BUFFALO (68 miles)—At this point we reach the Chicago & West Michigan road proper. The town itself is uninteresting, the stop being made only long enough to change engines.

We now, proceeding northward, enter the famous "fruit belt" of Michigan. On both sides may be seen great fields of small fruits, strawberries, raspberries, blackberries, etc., with miles of orchards, peaches, apples and pears, and vineyards, all in fine cultivation, until at last we reach the shipping center of it all, St. Joseph.

ST. JOSEPH (93 miles,) population 5000, situated at the mouth of the St. Joseph river. A long sandy beach stretches back from the water's edge for several hundred yards and is crowned by a bold bluff of sand along the edge of which is a driveway and park. Many beautiful views are to be enjoyed and "St. Joe" is fast becoming popular as a resort. Immense quantities of fruit are shipped annually from this port.

The St. Joseph river is pretty and is navigable for a number of miles to Berrien Springs. A number of pleasant summer hotels and boarding houses are found upon its banks. Steamers make regular daily trips, stopping at all the various "landings" en route.

The train, resuming the journey, crosses immediately the St. Joseph river to Benton Harbor on the opposite bank, then it continues through the fruit belt and some of the finest farming country in Michigan, to Holland.

HOLLAND (157 miles), population 8,000, one of the earliest Dutch settlements in Michigan, was founded by Albertus C. Von Raalte, "Dominie," in 1847. It is the seat of a Dutch Reform College and Theological Seminary with 200 students, and is a sturdy, thriving agricultural center. It is situated on the Black River which flows into Lake Michigan six miles west. At the mouth of the river are situated two resorts, Macatawa Park (south side), Ottawa Beach (north side). These resorts are popular and are reached by steam ferry boat from Holland or by a branch of railway from Waverly. Pleasant accommodations can be secured at reasonable rates.

The journey continues through an agricultural country similar to that already described, passing no points of special interest to Grand Rapids (179 miles).

GRAND RAPIDS—Population 100,000, one of the largest and most beautiful cities in Michigan, as well as one of the oldest. It was incorporated as a village in 1838 and as a city in 1850. It is situated in the beautiful valley of the Grand River, a stream of fair size and considerable importance both for navigation and water power, having a fall at Grand Rapids of eighteen feet. The city rises in fine elevations above the river. The streets are remarkably fine and abundantly supplied with beautiful shade trees and lined with handsome residences. A great deal of civic pride and enterprise has been shown, so that it stands in the front rank of modern municipal organizations.

Grand Rapids is pre-eminent for its manufacture of furniture, there being no less than 30 large firms engaged in this enterprise. It makes some of the finest furniture in the world, and has, in this respect, a more than national reputation. The value of these manufactories in 1890 was over twenty million dollars.

Grand Rapids also has extensive gypsum beds. A visit to the gypsum "mines" will be found very interesting and can be easily made. The mines or quarries of the Grand Rapids Plaster Co. are commended, as the gypsum is here mined by driving subterranean galleries into the bluff. Some of the color formations of the gypsum are very beautiful. Gypsum is a mineral substance (hydrated sulphate of lime) valuable for alabaster, plaster of Paris (so called because of the celebrated quarries at Mont Martre near Paris) and in agriculture for fertilizer. The alabaster qualities of the Grand Rapids gypsum are limited, but for all other purposes it is very valuable. The beds cover a range of from six to eight square miles in this vicinity and the supply is practically inexhaustible. Gypsum is found also in many other places in Michigan, especially in conjunction with salt deposits, but in smaller quantities. Geologically it belongs to the early Tertiary period.

b. Via Grand Rapids & Indiana Railway.

Grand Trunk Railway to Vicksburg.
212 miles; time 6¾ hours.

According to recent arrangements the Grand Rapids & Indiana trains now leave Chicago from the Polk street depot (State street car to Polk street, half block from depot). Leaving the depot the train soon crosses the state line into Indiana and traverses a rich agricultural district, passing en route the considerable cities of LaPorte and South Bend. The latter city is world famous for its manufactories of vehicles and agricultural implements.

Running northeast from South Bend the train enters Michigan near Cassopolis (122 miles) and reaches Vicksburg (151 miles) where it leaves the Grand Trunk Railway for the main line of the Grand Rapids & Indiana R. R. Thence it proceeds due north reaching Kalamazoo (163 miles).

KALAMAZOO (163 miles), population 21,000, one of the most beautiful cities in Michigan. It abounds in fine residences and churches, it is the center of many important manufactures—especially buggies—is the seat of a Baptist College and Presbyterian Ladies Seminary, both of high reputation. Kalamazoo is also famous for its celery, the soil of that region being especially adapted to the raising of this table delicacy. The growth is luxuriant and is unsurpassed in flavor and richness. One of the noted Insane Asylums of the world is located here, a state institution with property valued at one million dollars, caring for nearly 1200 inmates and employing seven medical attendants with 229 employes. Here the Grand Rapids & Indiana Railway crosses the Michigan Central R. R. Leaving Kalamazoo the road lies through a charming agricultural country to Grand Rapids (180 miles). For Grand Rapids see page 31.

II. From Detroit to Grand Rapids.

Travelers entering Michigan at Detroit or adjacent points, may take a route direct to Mackinaw City via the Michigan Central Railway, 291 miles, (see page 44) or may go to Grand Rapids and thence north, 379 miles. The latter is longer but has this advantage that it enters the resort region at its southern extremity, thus traversing en route much of the territory that would have to be afterwards reached should the traveler go direct to Mackinaw.

a. Via Grand Rapids & Western.

153 miles; time 4 hours.

Leaving Detroit from the fine Union Depot on Fort street, the train moves rapidly westward across a typical agricultural country, passing no places of special interest until Lansing is reached.

LANSING (88 miles), population 16,000, a pleasant city, the capital of the state and seat of several state institutions, chiefly the Agricultural College, the Boys' Industrial School and the Michigan School for the Blind. The conspicuous dome of the capitol building may be readily seen from the car window. The rest of the journey is uneventful and in one and a half hours (153 miles) Grand Rapids is reached. See page 31.

b. **Via Detroit, Grand Haven & Milwaukee R. R.**

158 miles; time 6 hours.

Leaving Detroit the journey is through an agricultural country all the way.

PONTIAC (26 miles), population 7,500, location of the Eastern Michigan Asylum for the Insane, an institution having a national reputation.

DURAND (67 miles), the junction point for several lines of railroad, but otherwise unimportant.

IONIA (124 miles), population 5,000, the location of the Michigan Asylum for Dangerous and Criminal Insane.

GRAND RAPIDS (158 miles). See page 31.

c. **Other Routes.**

Other though less usual northern routes should also be noted. The Michigan Central runs from Detroit to Grand Rapids via Jackson, 170 miles, 7¾ hours. The night train on this route will often be found of special convenience to westbound travelers. The Flint & Pere Marquette Railway from Toledo via Detroit, Flint, Saginaw, Reed City (where it connects with the Grand Rapids & Indiana Railway), Baldwin (where it connects with the Chicago & West Michigan R. R.) to Ludington. The Ann Arbor Railway from Toledo via Ann Arbor, Durand, Cadillac, (connecting here with the Grand Rapids & Indiana Railway see page 37), Thompsonville (where it connects with the Chicago & West Michigan R. R.) to Frankfort (see page 51).

III. From Grand Rapids to Traverse City, Petoskey & Mackinaw City.

a. Via Grand Rapids & Indiana Railway.

To Petoskey, 190 miles, time 6½ hours.
To Traverse City, 145 miles, time 5¼ hours.

Leaving Grand Rapids, the train almost immediately crosses the wide and rapid Grand River, skirts the city, crosses (3 miles) the Detroit, Grand Haven & Milwaukee R. R. and five minutes later passes on the right the extensive buildings of the fair grounds, passing en route numerous large furniture factories, the chief industry of this busy city. The train now follows closely the banks of the Grand River, affording numerous pretty vistas, to Belmont (10 miles), and crossing the Rogue River at Rockford, journeys through the well cultivated agricultural region to Howard City (34 miles).

At this point we enter the famous pine belt of Michigan. This whole region is the scene of the earliest of those great lumber enterprises which gave such impetus to the development of Michigan—indeed the whole northwest. The traveler will note with interest the fields of stumps, even yet incredibly thick, although many of them have been removed, which bear witness to the mighty forests of which they are the desolate remains. Great branching roots are piled up in stump fences about occasional clearings which, with the crude homesteader's "shanty" in the midst affords a unique picture of pioneer life—a picture which will not soon be forgotten by those who thus witness it for the first time. Numerous small towns with unpainted houses and inevitable little saw mill, are passed, and if the train stops interesting "studies" may be enjoyed of the various types of settlers that invariably gather at the depots to "see the train come in."

At Morley (41 miles) a small branch of the Muskegon is crossed. At Big Rapids (56 miles) a considerable town and the junction of the Detroit, Grand Rapids & Western Railway, the train crosses the Muskegon proper at about the center of its course. This river is one of the most important streams of Michigan. Taking its rise in Higgins Lake, 50 miles northeast of Big Rapids, it flows southwest to Muskegon and empties there into Lake Michigan. Thus as the bird flies it covers a course of over a hundred miles, but with its numerous bends and turns it has an actual course of fully twice that distance, and through the heart of a rich lumber district. It has, therefore, had an invaluable commercial importance, and the passing traveler hardly realizes the immense money value of the logs which have been floated on its waters to the great saw mills of Muskegon (see last paragraphs, page 37).

The train follows the river for several miles, passing at Paris (62 miles) on the left the pretty State Fish Hatchery where brook trout are "raised" for stocking the streams. Further on Reed City (69 miles) is reached, the junction with the Flint & Pere Marquette Railway (see page 34). The train now passes through a rough, uncultivated region of no special interest to the traveler, except as a type of pioneer country just emerging from its wilderness state into a condition of semi-cultivation. A number of very small hamlets are passed. The train reaches and skirts the shores of Clam Lake and stops at the largest and most important city thus far, Cadillac, (98 miles).

CADILLAC, a busy city of 8000 inhabitants, situated on the eastern shore of Little Clam Lake, a small but deep lake, two and a half miles long, connected by a short channel with the larger Clam Lake lying directly west. Cadillac is situated in the center of one of the richest tracts of pine ever known in the world, and has been the basis of lumber operations of great magnitude for more than twenty years.

Its large saw mills are still busy, although by far the greater part of the pine has been cut and much of the outlaying region is now a desolate waste. According to conservative estimates not more than 1,500,000 feet remains to be converted into lumber, a "cut" of less than five years. Immense tracts of virgin hardwood forests are, however, adjacent, and arrangements are being rapidly made to commence the manufacture of hardwood lumber. A fine boulevard has recently been constructed around the lake (8½ miles) and much civic enterprise is manifest.

The following statistics, furnished by courtesy of W. W. Mitchell, Esq., of Cadillac, will give some idea of the magnitude of lumber operations in this western section of Michigan.

During the last twenty-five years there has been manufactured in Muskegon, 10,040,670,500 feet; in Manistee, 5,498,228,666 feet; in Cadillac, 1,190,231,000 feet. The money value of this enormous amount may be easily computed by multiplying the above figures by four, "assuming that the average value of the timber standing during this period would range about $4.00 per thousand feet in the tree." Of course the manufactured product as it leaves the mill is worth from two to five times that amount.

This region was evidently a favorite rendezvous for

the Indians of prehistoric times. Along the shores of the lake are found numerous mounds, many of which have been excavated and much material of archeological value discovered. Those interested in this subject may correspond with Mr. Charles Manktellow of Cadillac, whose enthusiastic and painstaking researches along this line have resulted in "finds" of real value and importance.

Leaving Cadillac the train winding along high ridges and rounding sharp curves, affords a good view of the great pine barrens, which it almost immediately enters. Four miles north is the small junction, Missaukee, of a branch running to Lake City, a distance of 15 miles, and through an unbroken stretch of "barrens" as far as the eye can see on either side. For miles and miles this desolate wilderness of stumps stretches on either side with gaunt bare pine "stubs" sprinkled among them and decaying logs scattered in wild confusion everywhere. The stubby undergrowth of oak and poplar adds to, rather than relieves, the desolateness.

Passing through a country broken into billowy hills and ridges with sharp ravines, at six and a half miles from Cadillac the highest point of railroad land in Michigan is reached, known as Manton Hill, $832\frac{3}{4}$ feet above Lake Michigan. Here the road descends rapidly 477 feet in eleven miles to Manton and soon crosses the Manistee River. This is another of the notable streams of Michigan, over a hundred miles long and draining, with its tributaries, a large area. Down its currents also have been floated billions of feet of logs to be sawed into lumber at Manistee, which is situated at its mouth on the shores of Lake Michigan. A little later Walton Junction (119 miles) is reached.

From Walton Junction a branch road runs 26 miles to Traverse City with usually, in the summer time, through cars from Grand Rapids. The journey is through a country very similar to that already described. For Traverse City see page 57.

Continuing along the main line, the train, emerging from the forest, skirts the pretty shores of Fife Lake, and passing Fife Lake station (124 miles) crosses the south branch of the Boardman River at South Boardman. This river is famous as a trout stream.

The district now traversed consists of an extensive plain of jack pine, a small scrubby pine of rather picturesque appearance, but not commercially useful. Botanists will find this region of unique interest and a day may be very pleasantly spent in rambling among these dwarf trees at Kalkaska (138 miles), situated in the center of this region, a pleasant stopping place with a good hotel.

The road now rises steadily and sweeps through noble forests of elm, beech and maple which densely cover this great plateau. At Antrim (150 miles) an immense smelting works or "blast furnace" is passed, where iron ore from upper Michigan is converted into pig iron for commercial uses. The furnace is located here on account of the quantity of fire wood obtainable for burning, great fields of which, corded up, may be seen close by. A little further on is Mancelona (151 miles), one of the busiest towns between Cadillac and Petoskey.

The journey continues through almost unbroken forest, passing Alba with its charcoal kilns, and eight miles further on, at Elmira (166 miles), reaching the crest of another great ridge 663 feet above the level of Lake Michigan. Here begins a very rapid descent, the road grade having a fall of 572 feet in ten miles. In this distance twenty-one curves, aggregating 824° of curvature and 4½ miles, are made and it is interesting to watch the descent from the rear end of the train.

Descending the Elmira hill, the train enters the beautiful Boyne River valley. The hills slope abruptly down on either side covered with a noble forest, said to be the finest tract of hardwood in Michigan, whose greatest beauty is in the fall when the autumn colors are on. Boyne Falls is soon reached, where a little lumber railroad runs to Boyne City. For Boyne City see Part III, Sec. 2 Boyne Falls affords fine trout fishing. The Boyne River may also be reached from Boyne City.

The train now crosses a large and dense swamp of

tamarack and cedar, passing (7 miles) Bear Lake Junction, (see Part III, Sec 6). Saw mills are noted here and there. One of these mills finds sufficient cedar adjacent to produce twenty million shingles a year for twenty years. The little town of Clarion is passed, the grade rises steadily and soon Petoskey (191 miles) is reached.

For the journey from Petoskey to Mackinaw see Part III. Sec. 6.

6. Via Chicago & West Michigan Railway to Traverse City.

145 miles, 4 hours.

Leaving the Union Depot at Grand Rapids, the train skirts the city northward to the Detroit, Grand Haven & Milwaukee Junction (3 miles), with good views of the city en route. At 5 miles Mill Creek is passed, with the extensive fair grounds of the Michigan State Fair Association, and a little further on the right side the State Fish Hatchery, where black bass are raised for stocking the various lakes.

The route now lies through one of the famous fruit belts of Michigan, passing several prosperous towns, among these Sparta (15 miles) and Casnovia (22 miles). The latter town may be called the center of this fruit belt, large shipments of fruit—especially peaches—being made from this place each season.

The next stop of importance is Newaygo (36 miles). Just before reaching Newaygo we cross the Muskegon River, one of the most important streams in Michigan. (See page 36). Newaygo is a busy little town, a center of agricultural and lumbering pursuits.

Eleven miles further on is White Cloud (47 miles) on the White River, a junction point with a well known eating house. Trains usually stop twenty minutes for refreshment. Famous brook trout is served here in season.

Leaving White Cloud, the route lies for the most part through a wild and unsettled country. Here and there will be noted the rough "clearings" of the pioneer farmer. Great patches of forest and wide stretches of pine barrens are interspersed with little lakes and brawling streams whose waters afford splendid sport for the fisherman and the hunter.

At Roby's Tank, two and a half miles south of Baldwin and 73 miles from Grand Rapids, the Marquette River is crossed. This is a well known trout stream where the beautiful "rainbow trout" are found. The Club House situated here is open to the public and furnishes pleasant accommodations.

Baldwin (75 miles) is the junction point with the Flint & Pere Marquette R. R. From this point many fine trout streams may be be reached.

Eight miles north of Baldwin the train reaches the crest of Conley hill. From this point a superb view is secured. Following for several moments the crest of the hill or bluff, we look eastward over the tops of great trees away across the country for fifteen miles or more. The dense forests with their varied foliage, the fine prospect with its wide sweep of horizon afford a beautiful view. No better illustration can be had of the plateau-like conformation of the topography of Michigan. See Introduction, Sec. III and IV, also "Profile," page 25.

Two miles further on we reach Canfield, crossing a short railroad that extends to Luther, and three miles north of Canfield the train crosses the Little Manistee River. This is another famous trout stream, 13 miles from Baldwin, 88 miles from Grand Rapids. Good accommodations may be had here and fine fishing. Trains stop at all these streams and the accommodations preserve a remarkably high average.

Eight miles from this point the top of Norway Hill is reached. Descending this, the train passes for a short distance through a dense strip of Norway pine, giving the traveler beautiful glimpses of the forest vistas formed by this noble and graceful tree. At the foot of Norway Hill we pass Wellston, the site of an old lumber camp, and a little further on Boyne River is crossed, with good fishing and good accommodations.

Six miles further on we reach the high and picturesque banks of the Manistee River, another of the famous lumber streams of Michigan (see page 38). This river is crossed by an immense steel bridge. It is 1170 feet long, 90 feet high, and was built at a cost of $125,000.00.

The next stop is at Manistee Crossing (110 miles) where the Manistee and Northeastern R. R. crosses the Chicago & West Michigan Railway.

Entering a dense forest, the train crosses (5 miles) Bear River. Here, in the very heart of the woods, is a pleasant little hotel on the banks of the stream where again good fishing may be enjoyed.

Beyond this is Henry, the junction point with the "Betsy River and Arcadia R. R.," a logging railroad that reaches far into the forest. Then we pass the large charcoal kilns known as Desmonds, and one mile further on reach Thompsonville, a typical northern lumber village. Two and a half miles north of Thompsonville we cross the Betsy River. Good fishing. Then Wallin is passed, with its charcoal kilns, Clary with its stave mills, and Interlochen, all small lumber towns.

We are now fourteen miles from Traverse City.

Passing Bietner's we cross the Boardman River at Sabin, where is fine water power. The Traverse City Electric Light plant is located here. Good fishing. Later (141 miles) we reach Traverse City and find ourselves in the heart of the beautiful resort region of Michigan. For Traverse City see page 57 and for continuation of this route to Petoskey and Bay View see Part II, Sec. 4.

IV—From Detroit to Bay City, Cheboygan and Mackinaw City.

Via Michigan Central.

290 miles; time, 11 hours.

Travelers from Detroit will find it sometimes convenient to take the Michigan Central route to Mackinaw. The journey is through a country of little interest in scenic beauty; the night train, therefore, is most desirable. No cities of importance are passed, except Saginaw and Bay City, both large lumbering and mercantile centers.

Leaving Bay City (108 miles) the train enters what was once one of the famous Michigan lumber belts, although now by far the larger part has been cut.

Grayling (200 miles) was famous as a fishing region, but has lost its popularity in recent years.

At Indian River (256 miles) the road enters the resort region proper, skirting the beautiful shores of Mullet Lake for several miles, with stations at Topinbee (262 miles), Mullet Lake (268 miles) and Chebogan (274 miles). For particulars of these beautiful resorts see Part III, Sec. 6. Thence the road runs through dense forests of spruce, tamarack, hemlock and poplar to Mackinaw City (290 miles). For Mackinaw City see Part IV.

BY STEAMER.

Northern Michigan may also be reached by steamer direct from Chicago or Detroit. To many the novelty and charm of a trip on the Great Lakes is the crowning pleasure of a summer tour. Despite that *bete noire* of water travel, seasickness, there is a charm, restfulness and invigoration about such a voyage which appeals strongly to most tourists. Facilities of steamboat transportation are now so complete and perfect as to afford the highest degree of comfort, safety and pleasure. To those who enjoy the water and can spare the time (from twice to three times that required by rail) a voyage on the Great Lakes is strongly recommended. Warm wraps and overcoat should never be neglected. In the height of the season staterooms must be engaged several days, if not weeks, ahead.

I—From Chicago to Mackinac.

Two lines of steamers make regular trips between Chicago and Mackinac Island. The differences between them are so marked that they may be clearly stated without danger of invidious comparison. The Lake Michigan and Lake Superior Transportation Co. has in service the magnificent and palatial steamer Manitou. It is large, swift, and elegant in its appointments. It stops only at Charlevoix, Harbor Springs (passengers for Petoskey, 5 miles, are transferred here) and Mackinac

Island, and makes the trip in a little over twenty-four hours. The fare is $5.00, with meals, (served *a la carte* and with great elegance) and stateroom extra.

The Northern Michigan Line has in service two steamboats, the Petoskey and the Charlevoix. These boats have long been favorites. They have neither the speed nor elegance of the Manitou, but are very comfortable and less expensive. The fare is $7.00, meals and berth included. The service is plain and unpretentious. These boats make several stops en route, viz: Ludington, Manistee, Frankfort, Traverse City, Charlevoix, Petoskey, Harbor Springs and Mackinac Island. While this consumes much more time—about forty hours—it affords an opportunity to see much that is beautiful and interesting of Michigan coast scenery.

a. **Via Lake Michigan and Lake Superior Transportation Company.**

Passengers via the steamship Manitou steer their course directly up the lake and soon lose sight of land, which is not gained again until the Manitou Islands are sighted off the entrance to Grand Traverse Bay (see page 51). Further on north (30 miles) the Beavers are occasionally sighted. (See Part III, Sec. 2.) The course is now eastward to Charlevoix, where the first stop is made. The entrance to Charlevoix harbor, Round Lake, is both interesting and picturesque and should not be missed, even though it requires early rising to see it. Nothing can exceed the almost fairy-like beauty of this exquisite harbor, and the first impressions, as the stately boat passing through the narrow river sweeps about in beautiful Round Lake, will never be forgotten. For further description of Charlevoix, see Part III.

The passage to the open sea is then retraced and entering Little Traverse Bay the course is taken almost due east to Harbor Springs. Land is in sight on both sides, the shore rising in a series of beautiful, sweeping terraces, covered with dense forests, and reaching back to the blue distant hills. Little Traverse Bay is about ten miles long and five miles wide. It narrows at the end, to three miles, in a stately sweeping shore which rises in beautiful terraces from the bluff 100 feet high, like a great amphitheatre, and presents a scene of remarkable beauty. The deep blue, green and purple coloring of the water is fringed by snow-white lines of surf. Beyond gleams a beautiful white beach of sand or pebbles above which rise in many places sheer limestone bluffs bold and dark; then the land sweeps back in wide plateaus where dense forests contrast sharply with well-cultivated farms, the whole crowned by an imposing panorama of Petoskey and Bay View. Almost immediately the steamer enters the beautiful harbor. A long, narrow peninsula juts out into the lake inclosing a little bay, beyond which nestles Harbor Springs. This peninsula of singular beauty, is studded with fine summer homes with a picturesque little red brick lighthouse on the tip of the point. The water is very deep close to the shore, so that the largest steamers

sail within easy hailing distance of the lighthouse.

The harbor is practically land-locked and is exquisitely beautiful. Beyond the stretch of summer cottages lies the village, behind which rises an imposing wooded bluff fully 75 feet high. The whole effect is indescribably beautiful and the view from the steamer is only surpassed by the magnificent view secured from the bluff itself. (See Part III, Sec. 4.) Even if no longer stay is made, passengers shuld certainly not fail to climb the bluff. Conveyances at the dock may be secured for a very reasonable sum, and half an hour will be ample time for the round trip. The view thus enjoyed will never be forgotten. For details of Little Traverse Bay, with map, see Part III.

Leaving Harbor Springs the steamer retraces its course out of Little Traverse Bay, and bearing to the north, rounds "Nine Mile Point;" thence northward to the entrance of the Straits of Mackinac. On the right the shore line stands out in bold relief with high bluffs and gleaming beach of golden sand. The early and romantic settlement known as Cross Village may sometimes be discovered in the distance (about 25 miles by water from Harbor Springs, see Part III, Sec. 5) and beyond (15 miles) the long, low peninsula which guards the entrance to the Straits known as Waugoschance Point, with its reefs and tiny archipelago. To the left (but sometimes the steamers

clear this point far to the right) the little Isle Aux Galets (Flat-rock Island) appears with its tall lighthouse, which the natives pronounce "Skilly-ga-lee;" and a few miles farther north the large Waugoschance Island. Rounding this we are fairly in the far-famed Straits of Mackinac.

Now the course is almost due east to Mackinac Island. Fifteen miles brings the steamer off McGulpin's Point where the Straits narrow down to about five miles in width. To the north lies Point St. Ignace, the southern extremity of the upper peninsula; to the south lies Mackinaw City on the northern extremity of the lower peninsula, while immediately ahead (east) lies Mackinac Island with Round Island and Bois Blanc Island (pronounced "Bob-low") immediately below (see map Part IV). All this forms a panorama of magnificent proportions and beauty. The surf-crested shore, the blue water sparkling in the sun, the dark lying forests, the great white cliffs, the gleaming village and quaint old fortress, together with the constant procession of ships entering or leaving the Straits in either direction, combine to produce a view that is indescribably picturesque. The little white village of Mackinac nestling under its frowning crags adds an almost foreign touch to the beauty of the scene. Here we leave our boat to enter upon a more intimate inspection of the Island and its environs, a detail of which will be found in Part IV.

b. Via Northern Michigan Line.

If the steamers of the Northern Michigan line are taken, the course is held north by east from Chicago to Ludington, a prosperous and busy city of over 8000 population. Thence the shore is closely skirted (25 miles) to Manistee, where the second stop is made. Manistee is situated at the mouth of the Manistee River (see page 38) and is one of the largest lumber centers of Michigan. The steamer enters the river and sails slowly up the narrow channel, about a quarter of a mile, to the dock. On leaving it goes on up the river into Manistee Lake, where a busy scene is presented. The lake is lined with saw mills, its docks are crowded with lumber in massive piles, and its waters covered with logs held in place by "booms," i. e. great strings of logs chained or roped together. The drivers show marvelous skill in walking these logs and in maneuvering them about and sorting them. Here the steamer finds room to turn about. It swings around and steams slowly down the river and out again to sea.

Once more the course is northward, usually in sight of shore, whose varying scenery is full of novelty and pleasure to the traveler. The next stop is Frankfort. Here the steamer enters a short, narrow river and then a charming little lake. The quiet beauty of this graceful harbor impresses one at once and it is left always with a little sigh of regret. Frankfort is the terminus of the Ann Arbor Railway and the point of departure of its line of steamers to Menominee, Manitowoc and other points across the lake.

Leaving Frankfort, the steamer soon veers a little to the east, passing, in about an hour, the quite imposing Sleeping Bear Point. This great promontory is made of gleaming white sand and rises to a height of nearly 500 feet; it is crowned with patches of scrubby pine and spruce. Almost directly north, about 12 miles, lie the Manitou Islands, the larger one rising abruptly from the water in cliffs 200 feet high. The course now lies northeast up the long peninsula which lies between the lake and Traverse Bay, known as Leelanaw Peninsula, about 35 miles, when rounding Lighthouse Point we turn sharply down this imposing bay to Traverse City (30 miles). Passing on the west Northport and Omena we soon enter the narrow west arm, and enjoying the beautiful shores with their thickly-wooded hills and pretty villas, we reach the dock at Traverse City. For details of Grand Traverse Bay with maps, see Part II.

Leaving Traverse City, the steamer returns up the bay, and rounding the main land seventeen miles northeast of Lighthouse Point, enters Charlevoix (about 45 miles from Traverse City.) For a description of the reminder of the trip see page 47. For Charlevoix and environs, see Part III.

II—From Detroit to Mackinac.

a. **Via Northern Steamship Company.**
b. **Detroit & Cleveland Steam Navigation Co.**

Travelers from Detroit may reach Mackinac Island by steamer on lines indicated above. (The twin steamers of the Northern Michigan line, the Northwest and Northland, are magnificent boats. Their exceptional size, speed and beauty demands this special notice. They are exclusively for passenger service, and plying between Buffalo and Duluth, stop at Cleveland, Detroit, Mackinac Island and Sault Ste. Marie en route. Time from Buffalo to Duluth, 3 days; from Detroit to Mackinac Island, 20 hours.) The voyage is somewhat longer, and aside from the trip between Detroit and Port Huron, is practically out of sight of land. Detroit River always presents an animated scene, an immense volume of traffic being carried through its waters—over thirty-six million tons in a single season.

At its mouth it is four miles wide, but narrows to about a mile between Detroit and Windsor. Passing Belle Isle, a beautiful park of 700 acres, the boat enters Lake St. Clair, a wide and shallow lake about twenty-five miles in diameter. The marshes about this lake are famous hunting and fishing grounds. The lake is connected with Lake Huron by the St. Clair River, forty miles long, and presents many charming vistas. At its entrance lies Port Huron, connected with Sarnia by the famous tunnel of the Grand Trunk Railway. This tunnel is 1½ miles in length and is considered one of the finest executions of engineering skill. It is a great cast-iron tube, or series of tubes, twenty feet in diameter, and cost $2,700,000.

Leaving the St. Clair River the steamer traverses the whole length of Lake Huron (270 miles) without a stop, though often in sight of the Michigan shore. At last Bois Blanc Island (pronounced "Bob-low") is reached the narrow channel between it and the mainland bending abruptly into the Straits of Mackinac. For description of Straits see page 50. For Mackinac Island with map see Part IV.

PART II.

GRAND TRAVERSE BAY.

1. Traverse City and Immediate Environs.

TRAVERSE CITY—One of the principal cities of northern Michigan, finely located on the south west end of Grand Traverse Bay and in a country rich in agricultural and lumber resources.

HISTORY— Traverse City was incorporated as a city in 1895 and as a village in 1881. Previous to that time it was a well known rendezvous in early Indian and pioneer days. Situated deep in the lower end of a great bay, it was out of the line of general travel from Canada to the Mississippi, and therefore failed to play any important part in the stirring history of colonial times. But the quiet retirement and natural beauty of its situation made it a most attractive place for Indian camping grounds, while its great resources, beautiful harbor and fine water power privileges combined to make it a place of large commercial importance the natural site for a prosperous city.

We know that in the early days a small Indian village occupied this site. At that time the Boardman River flowed, clear as crystal, with a fine curve to the lake, the great pines swept in a noble forest to the very shore and all nature contributed to make this place a singularly charming spot.

In 1847 Capt. Boardman, of Illinois, came here and purchased a large tract of land from the government, and under great difficulties, with energy and perseverance succeeded in building up a little settlement with saw mill, postoffice and other essentials of early pioneer life. In 1891 he sold out all his interest to the firm of Hannah, Lay & Co., then young men, who at once began the making of a city and to whose sagacity and indomitable energy much of the present prosperity of Traverse City is due.

Thirty years after this purchase Traverse City, growing as a center for lumber, agriculture and manufacturing, was incorporated as a village, and in 1895 as a city, having a present population (in 1898) of more than 6000.

Traverse City has developed manufacturing industries of large proportions. Some statistics may be of interest. The Oval Wood Dish Co. employs 350 persons and puts out a half million dishes per day, besides manufacturing clothes pins, washboards and other articles of woodenware. The Basket Factory made three and a half million grape baskets and five million peach baskets in the eight months of last year, besides many thousands of other kinds of baskets. In addition to these the Chair Stock Factory and the Potato Implement Factory do a large business, not to speak of numerous other industries of similar nature. Traverse City is also a center for shipping fruit which this region produces in great abundance. Apples, plums and small fruits, and an almost incredible quantity of potatoes are shipped from this port to all parts of the country.

ITINERARY—Situated on the edge of the bay, the business interests of Traverse City are stretched along one long street running parallel with the water. The city is also broken by the curves of the Boardman river. Back of the main street lies the residence portions, on both sides of the river, while behind these one enters immediately the beautiful pineries whose open forests have a never-failing charm. Still farther back are high bluffs (2 miles), a very pleasant walk, (in which the Asylum may be included) affording a beautiful view of the city, the river, Boardman Lake—a pretty inland lake offering many attractive recreations—with the bay, its islands, peninsulas and charming coast line.

The Asylum is a point of special interest. It is open to visitors and should certainly be inspected. The Northern Michigan Asylum was organized in 1881 and opened in 1885 under the support and control of the government of Michigan. Its imposing buildings stand in a beautiful park of spacious dimensions immediately below the bluffs surrounding the city on the southwest. The property consists of fifteen buildings with 588 acres; it has a present value of over $775,000. It has, at present, 553 male inmates and 460 female—a smaller number than in previous years. The disbursements for the year ending June 30th, 1896, which include special extra appropriations, were $206,646. The receipts for the same year were $195,811. There are five medical attendants beside the Superintendent, and 172 employes.

The roads about Traverse City are exceptionally good. Beautiful walks, drives and bicycle rides may be enjoyed in every direction. Some of the most important of these are described in detail in the pages immediately following. Those interested will find a visit to the various manufactories full of profit and pleasure. The plan of the city is so simple as to require no special directions or explanations.

2. From Traverse City to Northport.

THE LEELANAW PENINSULA.

A glance at the map will reveal the simple yet interesting topography of this section. Grand Traverse Bay forms a deep indentation in the sweeping shore line of the great lake. Its western coast is a long, pointed peninsula, known as Leelanaw County. The bay itself is divided, in its southern extremity, by another small, narrow peninsula, which, piercing its center, extends northward for about eighteen miles, making two lower bays known as West Arm and East Arm. Beyond, on the east, sweeps the shore of the mainland northward to Elk Rapids and Charlevoix. Three natural divisions are thus made consisting of two peninsulas, Leelanaw and Old Mission, and the coast of the mainland.

The most northern settlement of Leelanaw peninsula is Northport. It may be reached by steamboat daily from Traverse City, forming, in fine weather, a delightful day's excursion of about sixty miles including the return trip. Sailing up the bay the steamer pauses at Ne-ah-ta-wan-ta (see page 64), Omena (see page 62) and Northport. It may also be reached by carriage road, a delightful journey of forty miles. The tourist will vary the trip to suit his own tastes, but our description, for the sake of completeness, covers the whole journey by road, either for driving, bicycle or pedestrian.

Leaving Traverse City the road lies along the shore for almost fifteen miles. Traverse Beach (7 miles from Traverse City) is first reached—a pretty resort with charming hotel. Still following the shore, we reach, about four miles further on, a place where a road turns to the left climbing a rather steep hill. This will lead us to the old road, but recently a new and more desirable road has been built straight on along the shore for nearly seven miles further, to where the shore runs out in a beautiful little bay to Lee's Point.

At Lee's Point one may secure a very fine view, but unless it is desired to lengthen the journey by several miles, it would be well to omit this, and continuing due north leave the shore for a time and cross the headland straight to Sutton's Bay, about four miles. On reaching the shore we round the bay, and in less than two miles reach Sutton's Bay postoffice, a small hamlet, making in all about 24 miles from Traverse City. At this point a beautiful road runs nearly due west to (5 miles) Carp Lake, to Provemont and Fountain Point (see page 63.)

Continuing the journey to Northport, the road follows closely the shore, affording most beautiful views all the way, about nine miles to Omena—a picturesque and interesting Indian village. The village lies in a pretty cove close to the shore. Above rises a high bluff upon which is situated the large Leelanaw hotel with beautiful grounds and affording magnificent views. The history of Omena is closely connected with that of Old Mission, across the west arm of the bay. In connection with the missionary and educational work organized at Old Mission (for which see page 65), a station was established here in 1852. This philanthropy was conducted by the Presbyterian Church as one of its mission enterprises for many years. The old church still remains in the center of the quaint little village and the Indians meet regularly here for worship under the pastoral care of the Rev. J. Payson Mills. From Omena to Northport is seven miles by a most beautiful and picturesque road, passing en route the old Indian town of Ah-go-sa, named after an Indian chief of early repute.

Northport, a little village of 600 inhabitants, is the outpost of Leelanaw peninsula. Its history marks the beginning of the white settlement of Leelanaw County. In 1849 the Rev. Geo. N. Smith removed with a tribe of

Indians from Holland, Mich., to this country. He was in company with James McLaughlin, a government employe—as government farmer for a band of Waukazoo Indians from Allegan county. They set sail from Holland, May 27th, 1849, and after a tempestuous voyage, reached Cat Head Bay, just north of Northport on the main lake coast, June 11th. A little later Northport was chosen as the permanent location, and with forty or fifty Indian families who also migrated here, quite a settlement was immediately formed. In 1854 Messrs. Fox & Rose began extensive operations here, building the first dock for large steamers in Grand Traverse Bay. Mr. H. O. Rose of this firm is now a resident of Petoskey.

Beyond Northport the peninsula stretches northward for more than seven miles, to Lighthouse Point. Bicyclers and pedestrians of an exploring turn of mind, will find the trip interesting. As the peninsula now narrows down to a slender strip of land, no special directions will be needed.

From Northport the return journey may be made, if desired, by a different route, coming by way of Carp Lake. The road runs in angular route across the peninsula to the head of Carp Lake, and thence rounding the lake, follows a narrow strip of land between Carp Lake and Lake Michigan to Leland, an interesting though rather deserted village. Here a little steamer may be taken, traversing Carp Lake and stopping at Fountain Point, Provemont, a resort with a fine artesian well over thirty years old, and other places of interest and beauty to Fuch's hotel, the southern extremity of the lake. Here the Manistee & Northeastern R. R. makes connection for Traverse City. Or the journey may be completed by carriage road (somewhat hilly) to Traverse City—a distance of 12 or 13 miles.

Carp Lake offers fine sport for the fisherman, and it may be said in general that this whole region is charming and beautiful. No more delightful trip could be planned, full of novel sights and experiences, than the one just outlined. It can be easily made by wheel or carriage, in three days, by using steamboat and railroad connections, in shorter time, while many days can be most happily spent in wandering about this charming peninsula.

3. From Traverse City to Old Mission.

OLD MISSION PENINSULA.

While there is no regular boat route from Traverse City to Old Mission, some of the steamers occasionally touch there—inquire at hotel. The round trip by carriage road is very beautiful and may be easily made in a day by carriage or bicycle. Old Mission peninsula is about eighteen miles long and from one to five miles in width. It is a veritable garden, being all under cultivation. Some of the finest fruit orchards in Michigan are on this peninsula.

The road lies westward from Traverse City a short distance, and then north along the shore to Bower's Harbor in the bight of a little bay about twelve miles from Traverse City. Here a road follows the shore for two miles to Traverse Point and Ne-ah-ta-wan-ta, both beautifully located summer resorts of considerable proportions. Directly south of Traverse Point lies the beautiful Marion Island, and close by a little island known as Hermit Island inhabited solely by an eccentric old fisherman and hunter.

The main road to Old Mission, however, turns inland about a mile before reaching Bower's Harbor, and runs due north for about six miles through beautiful orchards; hence turns westward at right angles for about a mile to Old Mission, finely situated on a little bay opening into the east arm.

Old Mission is one of the historic landmarks of this region. In May, 1839, two Presbyterian missionaries, Revs. John Flemming and Peter Dougherty, came to this spot by canoe from Mackinac Island to establish a mission among the Indians settled here. They brought supplies with them, including doors and windows for a house. A council of the Indians was called and it was first thought best to locate at Elk Rapids, just across the bay. A beginning was made here. Mr. Flemming returned to Mackinac in a few weeks on account of the sudden death of his wife. Mr. Dougherty was left alone, the only white man in the region. A month later he returned to Old Mission for consultation with Henry R. Schoolcraft, Indian Agent at Mackinac. Old Mission was then chosen as the location of the enterprise. The station at Elk Rapids was abandoned and moving to Old Mission, Mr. Dougherty lived there for many years conducting missionary, industrial and educational work among the Indians of great value and importance. In 1852 (about 13 years later) the mission work was moved to Omena (see page 62).

The journey may now be resumed by returning down the shore of east bay due south to Fowlers (6 miles), beautiful views all the way, and then angling across the narrow neck of the peninsula to Traverse City, twelve miles further.

4. Traverse City to Charlevoix and Petoskey.

I. By Rail, C. & W. M. R. R.

Charlevoix, 1¾ hours, 62 miles.
Petoskey, 2½ hours, 75 miles.

Leaving Traverse City the train crosses Boardman River and skirts the East Arm Bay to Acme. Hence deflecting to the west, the first stop is made at Williamsburg. This is the junction point for a branch of the road which runs to Elk Rapids (see page 72), trains making close connections. Beyond Williamsburg the next stop is Barker Creek, where on the left, across a cedar swamp, Round Lake may be seen. This is one of that beautiful chain of lakes which extends almost the whole of the distance to Charlevoix, along whose picturesque shores the railroad runs to Ellsworth.

The next stop is made at Van Buren. Torch River lies two miles west and carriages from Welch's Inn meet passengers here. Immediately crossing Rapid River, the fine expanse of Torch Lake soon bursts into view, and we follow closely the shore for several miles to the pretty village of Alden. Leaving Alden, the road follows the lake shore for about three miles, then turning abruptly eastward, skirts Clam Lake, a little connecting lake or more properly river. We get only occasional glimpses of this lake, when turning northward, again, the train, crossing numerous babbling trout streams, rapidly skirts the western edge of Grass Lake and plunges into the forest for a mile or so, stopping at Bellaire, a pretty little lumber town situated on the narrows between Grass and Intermediate Lakes.

At Bellaire the train crosses the narrows or river and the view is on the right hand side of the car for the rest of the way. Occasional glimpses of the river are caught until, emerging from the woods, we come out

upon the southern shore of Intermediate Lake with a tiny island in the center of the channel. The train skirts the shores of this beautiful lake for miles. The forest is very dense and grand, being heavy hardwood timber. The shores rise in steep terraces abruptly from the lake, the water reflects as in a mirror the beautiful foliage, and the whole journey is one constant panorama of extensive vistas of water, forest and hillside.

The next stop is at Central Lake, another industrious little town. After following the lake along its now narrow course—more like a river than a lake—the road skirts a sort of bayou and then leaving the water altogether, plunges for a few moments into a dense forest whose noble foliage cannot but command our admiration. In a few moments once more the lake appears, seemingly more beautiful than ever because of the splendid opposite bank which rises in a graceful slope to considerable height and is covered with noble trees. All along the lake lumber operations are noted. Here a tug towing logs and there a raft; now a skiff and now a little camp upon the shore. Not for an instant does the scene lose its charm until, with a sigh of regret, we reach Ellsworth, which marks the head waters of this beautiful chain of lakes—though to speak accurately, the lake makes a broad bend here and continues its course for several miles further in a southeasterly direction.

Ellsworth is a small village and the connecting point with a stage line (7 miles) to East Jordan. East Jordan is also reached by boat from Charlevoix (see page 85).

As if to atone for the disappointment on leaving Intermediate Lake, our route leads us past three other pretty little lakes about whose shores the railroad winds until at last the large and handsome Pine Lake appears on the right. This we skirt for a mile, stopping first at Belvedere, a station close to the Belvedere Hotel of the Kalamazoo resort in Charlevoix. Then crossing the narrow channel between Round and Pine Lakes, the train stops at the Charlevoix depot proper. To the left is the new, large and handsome Charlevoix Inn with its beautiful grounds. To the right the pretty depot park stretches to the water's edge. For Charlevoix see page 79.

The journey now lies through rather a desolate looking country, the scene in recent years of fierce forest fires, for a few miles. Occasional glimpses of Lake Michigan may be had to the left (north side). The pretty resort Bay Shore is passed and again we enter the woods, and in a few minutes emerge upon the very shores of the great lake itself. This forms one of the finest approaches to Petoskey. The view is superb. We are fully a hundred feet above the water, on the very edge of the bluff. Before us stretches the great lake; straight across (9 miles) lies the opposite bank of Little Traverse Bay, which sweeps eastward to Bay View and Petoskey. A little to the east the pretty lighthouse may be plainly seen on a clear day, marking Harbor Springs. Away in front of us in the bight of the bay the shore rises in fine bluffs crowned with the cottages of Roaring Brook and Bay View. The

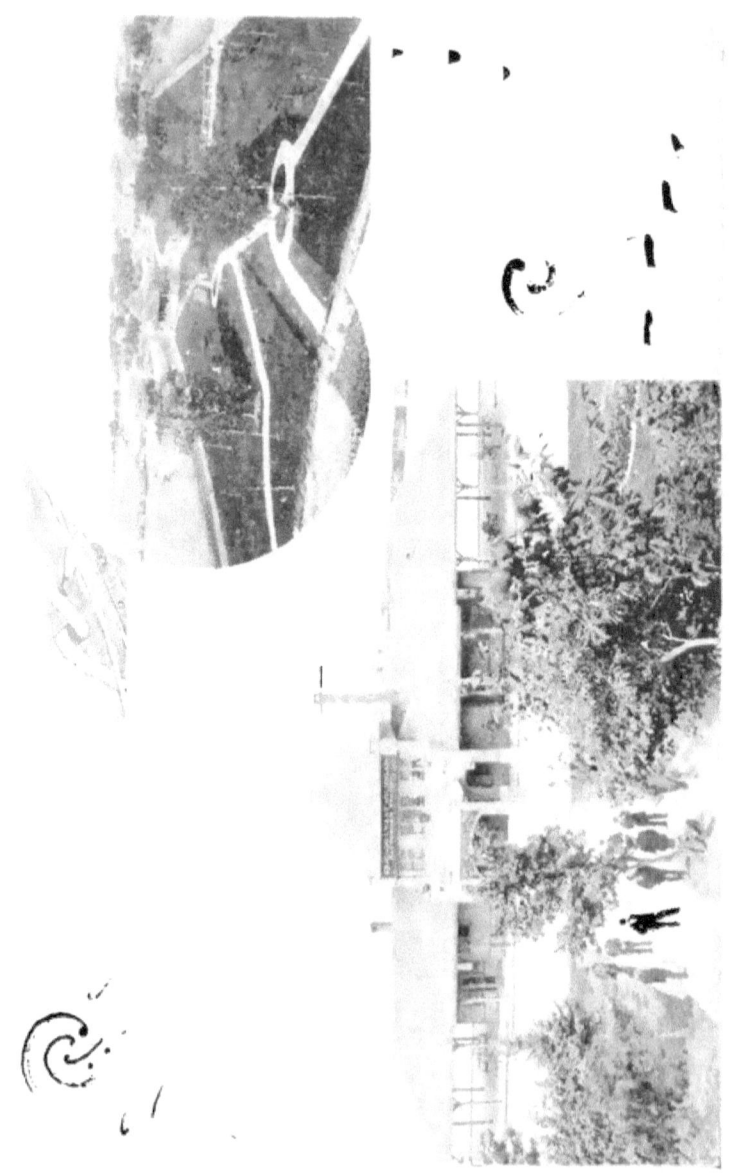

C. & W. M. DEPOT, PETOSKEY.

large white building directly ahead is the New Arlington Hotel, while below us the water glows in matchless colors or dances in golden ripples, or dashes in pure white surf against the beautiful beach. Meanwhile the train is rapidly descending the bluff and rounding a pretty point, crosses the brawling Bear Creek, to stop at the handsome Petoskey depot. From thence it proceeds close along the shore of the bay, past the imposing limestone quarry (see page 99) to its terminus at Bay View.

2. By Carriage Road to Elk Rapids and Inland Lakes to Charlevoix.

The trip from Traverse City to Elk Rapids may be made by carriage road and will afford a pleasant drive or bicycle ride. The road is, in general, in good condition and for many long stretches very fine. It is somewhat hilly in the central portion, the hills being long but not steep. The distance is eighteen miles and many fine views are to be enjoyed.

Crossing the Old Mission peninsula, the road follows along the bay immediately above the railroad, which it crosses at Acme (4 miles). From this point it runs nearly due north, with occasional glimpses of the lake, through a fine farming country passing (about 13 miles) a little lake on the right known as Lake Pto-ba-go. Soon we climb a hill whose crest reveals a fine expanse of lake and shore line. The character of the country from this point begins to show a marked change. Long and beautiful hedges of spruce and fir, wide "openings" adorned with the low, flaring and circular juniper—a shrub or bush of the evergreen family—and exquisite copses of small pines take the place of fields and farms. The road is from this point (for five miles), to Elk

Rapids, exceptionally fine and the whole scene is one of wild, romantic beauty and delightful interest to the visitor.

ELK RAPIDS—A little town, finely situated on the west shore of Grand Traverse Bay where Elk Lake, and its long chain of sister lakes, flows into Lake Michigan. The rapids, headed in recent years by a large dam, takes its course so as to form a pretty island crowned with a handsome residence and park. The town itself is neatly laid out, a typical small lake port, and will be full of interest to the observant traveler. It has a very good hotel and is headquarters for boating and fishing excursions of great variety and interest.

A small steamer leaves Elk Rapids every day to traverse for some distance, the chain of inland lakes which lie behind it. The route is very pretty. No more delightful trip can be imagined than to take a small boat, row or sail, and follow the course of these lakes to their head waters at Ellsworth. Such a trip has many advantages—perfect safety, great variety and beauty of scenery, fine fishing of every kind, and in addition to these the route passes so many little towns, not to mention farm houses, that one is in constant and easy reach of good accommodations. It may be made long or short, according to desire, by use of railroad and steamboat facilities along the way. A good row boat fitted with a small sail is recommended for such a trip. While of course reasonable familiarity with the handling of a boat is necessary, expert knowledge is not required as the lakes are so narrow and landlocked that danger from storms is reduced to the slightest minimum. By use of the map (see page 56) and a little care, a guide is unnecessary.

The course lies across Elk Lake from Elk Rapids to the narrows leading into Round Lake. Note that the passage is not in the extreme bight of the bay, but a little above. By taking at once the east shore it cannot be missed. Rounding this shore, we soon enter Torch River, a pretty stream in the center of whose course is located Welch's hotel. A little above the hotel the Rapid River, a famous trout stream, pours into Torch River. Continuing our course, we enter Torch Lake, and, taking at once the east bank, Alden, a pretty village, is passed about four miles, and six miles further north we reach the entrance of Clam Lake. Torch Lake itself stretches away northward for twelve miles to

Eastport. Many pleasant places are located on the upper shores of this lake.

Entering Clam Lake, we follow a narrow, winding course through Clam Lake and up the east shore to Grass Lake. At its northern edge (a long arm to the west to be avoided) we enter the narrows, and in two miles reach Bellaire. Here the stream is very narrow, and a mill dam is reached where portage must be made. The mill owners are required by the laws of river navigation to make this portage for all boats, and a courteous request for assistance to the foreman, will be promptly responded to. A little difficulty may be experienced with logs on the upper stream, but reasonable assistance will always be given by the mill men. A little patience and judgment will surmount all obstacles.

Passing through the beautiful Intermediate River (keep east bank and avoid long bayou on the west) we enter Intermediate Lake. This lake is a gem of beauty; it resembles a river, being long and narrow. The banks rise high on either side, covered with noble forests and grand foliage. It is nearly fifteen miles from the mouth of the narrows to Ellsworth, where the head waters are reached. Ellsworth being on the railroad, the boat may be sent back from this point to its proper destination by freight. To those who enjoy a cruise of this sort, we know of no more charming or feasible route. Compare, however, the Inland Route (page 128), which may be made the entire way by steamer if so desired.

From Elk Rapids bicyclers may continue the journey to Charlevoix, following due north between Torch Lake and Grand Traverse Bay to the village of Torch Lake (about 13 miles); hence north to the extremity of Torch Lake to Eastport (3 miles); hence due north eight miles, passing the little town of Atwood, five miles from Eastport. From this point the road travels in angular direction northeast, nine miles to Charlevoix. While the journey may be readily made, the road can not be called first class and the bicyclist must be prepared to do some hard riding.

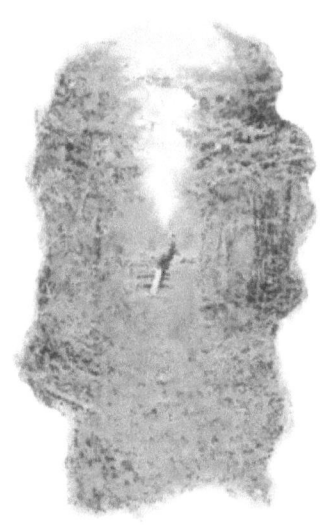

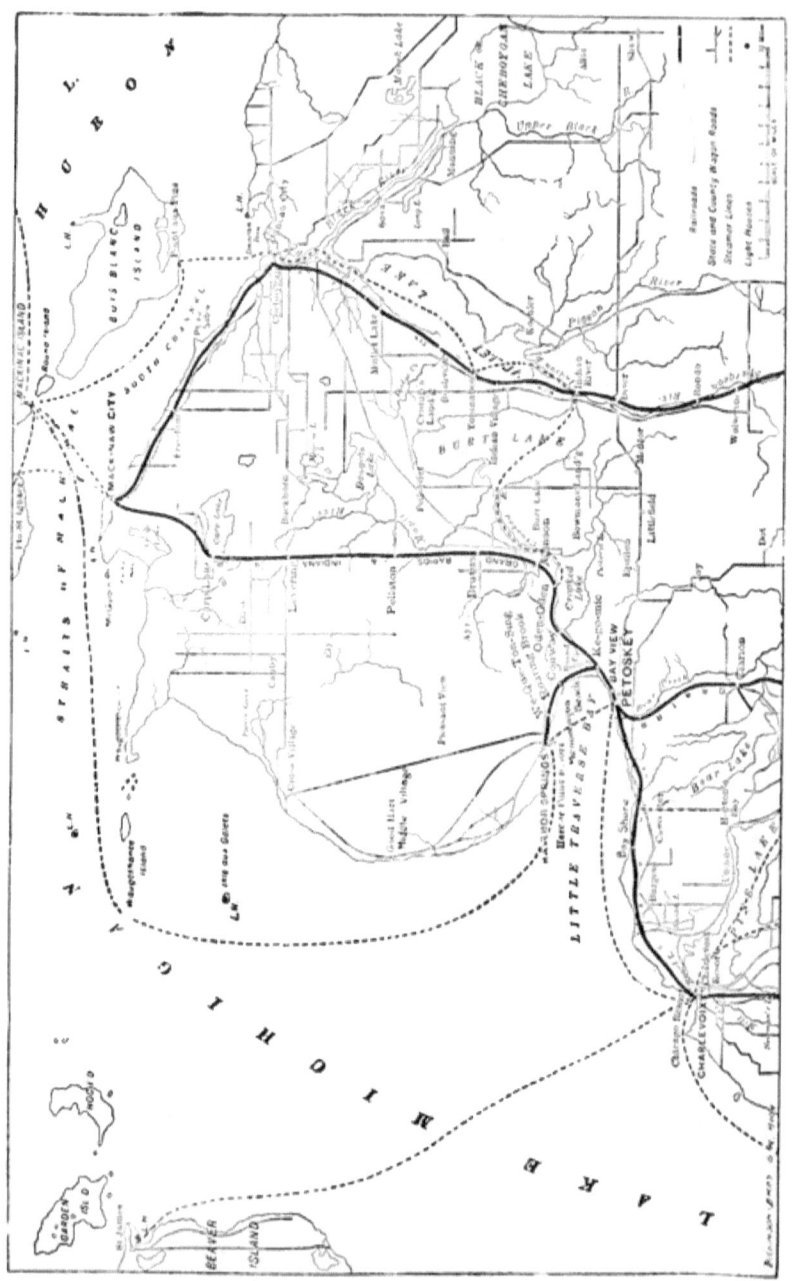

LITTLE TRAVERSE BAY.

PART III.

LITTLE TRAVERSE BAY.

Immediately above Grand Traverse Bay the shore of the mainland begins to recede in a bold headland toward the east. At this point lies Charlevoix, which may be called the entrance to Little Traverse Bay, although technically the bay really begins several miles further eastward. This bay is much smaller than Grand Traverse Bay, but its position, beauty and varied attractions have made it famous among the summer resorts of the country. It is about 20 miles from Charlevoix to Petoskey, and the bay varies in width from nine to three miles. A description as approached by steamboat will be found on page 47.

1. Charlevoix.

(1) HISTORY—The history of Charlevoix is intimately related to that of the whole region of which it is a part. Its strategic situation upon a headland commanding the entrance to both great bays, gave it importance as a place of rendezvous on the main thoroughfare of early Indian and pioneer travel. Its marvelous beauty and perfect adaptation for camping purposes made it a favorite stopping place. Its river, with beautiful Round Lake, opening up into Pine Lake, gave it commercial importance of great value. Nature certainly has lavished here every gift of grace and beauty, and it is a matter of sincere congratulation

that commercial and utilitarian interests have been able to destroy so little of its original unique and surpassing charm.

Aside from its occasional mention as a stopping place for the earliest pioneers, Charlevoix's chief historic interest lies in its connection with the Mormon "kingdom," a full account of which is narrated on page 89. The center of Mormon operations was Beaver Island, but a place of such importance strategically as Charlevoix could scarcely escape the covetous desires of these early "pirates", as they have well been called. Previous to 1850 Charlevoix, or Pine River as it was then known, had been inhabited by numerous fishermen, and quite a little settlement had gradually grown up. These were the victims of constant depredations by the Mormons of Beaver Island, and many sharp quarrels resulted. In 1852 a party of Mormons, attempting to secure the persons of three fishermen through some legal technicalties, were met by armed resistance when they landed at Charlevoix. Shots were exchanged on both sides and several of the Mormons wounded. The party withdrew with threats of vengeance, and the fishermen, fearing later attacks by a stronger party, left in a panic, deserting their homes and much of their property. After this occurrence the place was occupied by Mormon squatters for some years.

In 1855 Mr. John S. Dickson arrived. He had purchased a large tract of land here from the State. A long, unhappy struggle with the Mormons ensued, and many thrilling tales are recorded of his experiences and those of his wife, who at one time was forced to leave her children and walk the whole distance to Petoskey along the shore, with no road, to summon aid against a Mormon attack. These piratical depredations did not end until the assassination of Strang in 1856 and with his death the breaking up of the Mormon settlement on Beaver Island. From that time the village grew undisturbed, passing through all the experiences incident to a pioneer settlement, until 1879 when it was incorporated as a village. In recent years it has been specially

attractive as a place of summer resort, while its connection by water with a large interior region has made it always a shipping port of considerable importance. It has a population of nearly 2,000.

(2) ITINERARY—Charlevoix is so located as to present a view exceptionally charming and offering an

unusual variety of summer attractions. The coast of Lake Michigan consists at this point of a series of sand dunes or hills which follow a small but sharp indentation in the shore. Between these sand dunes, (the tallest is known as Mount McSauba) the Pine River cuts its narrow channel. This has been so improved by the Government as to provide a channel for the largest boats, and its entrance is marked by a small lighthouse at the end of a long breakwater. The river proper is quite narrow and less than half a mile long, opening into beautiful little Round Lake. Here where the banks sweep in terraces down to the water's edge, nestles the little village, and all about are grouped the charming summer homes of the various resorts. For this reason it is difficult to determine upon any single starting point for our itinerary.

Perhaps the most convenient will be the swinging bridge which crosses the river just at the entrance to Round Lake and close to the steamer docks. From this bridge one gets a good view of the main business street of the town. Our first stroll will take us through this street to the foot of a hill (about three blocks) where, turning to the left we follow the fine avenue to the Kalamazoo resort and Bellvedere hotel. Pretty cottages adorn the beautiful terraces upon the right, while on the left the lake glows in a deep and beautiful blue. Across upon the other shore are seen the handsome cottages of the Chicago resort. Beyond, the lake rounds to a narrow stream, across which is thrown the large iron railroad swinging bridge. Following the avenue to its end (about five minutes walk) we reach the attractive Bellvedere hotel surrounded with cottages, and beyond, across the railroad track, the wide and fine expanse of Pine Lake lies before us.

Pine Lake is a large sheet of water divided, at the southern extremity, into two arms—South Arm, leading to East Jordan (12 miles); and Pine Lake proper, ending in Boyne City, about 15 miles from Charlevoix. Turning to the right, the cottages extend back of the hotel for a considerable distance, and immediately across the street is the little suburban depot of the Chicago & West Michigan R. R. known as Bellvedere. From this point the railroad bridge may be crossed by those in haste (crossing unpleasant and dangerous) to the Charlevoix Inn and depot proper which lie immediately across the river (a row boat may sometimes be secured as ferry).

Most visitors will, however, prefer to retrace the journey through the village, and returning to the bridge, climb the little hill that lies beyond, and passing through a pretty residence portion of Charlevoix, take the first turn to the right. Follow this street for five minutes walk when the beautiful new Charlevoix Inn, which graces the shores of Pine Lake, appears to the right. The Inn is 450 feet long, built on graceful lines, situated in a beautiful park with fine approach from the depot. Beyond the depot the pretty railroad park stretches to the water's edge. Immediately across the track is located a natatorium, complete and elegant in all its appointments. The Charlevoix Inn, completed in 1898, is one of the most elegant and beautiful of the hotels of American summer resorts and should certainly be inspected by the tourist.

Just before reaching the hotel a large greenhouse is passed; turning at this point to the left (north) a footpath (5 minutes walk) leads to the conspicuous Mount McSauba upon which an observatory tower has been built. From this commanding eminence a view of surpassing beauty may be enjoyed. The itinerary will be completed by descending from this point to the shore of Lake Michigan, and following that shore through charming grove and beach back to the river, thence past the Fountain House to the swinging bridge, our point of beginning.

ROUND LAKE furnishes ideal boating and bathing privileges and pleasant outings, both rowing and sailing, may be enjoyed. Competent sailors may be secured at very reasonable cost and a cruise under their direction in Round and Pine Lakes will be found a most delightful recreation. The tourist can vary his enjoyments almost indefinitely to suite his tastes and time.

2. Excursions from Charlevoix.

1 **Pine Lake.**

As has been previously noted, Pine Lake is an extensive sheet of water, fifteen miles long and averaging about three miles wide. It is divided at the southern extremity by a blunt peninsula, the South Arm bay being long and narrow. Steamers leave about once in two hours for the two principal ports at the extremities of the lake, East Jordan and Boyne City. The round trip is very enjoyable and may be made in six hours. Leaving the dock at Charlevoix, the little steamer crosses Round Lake, and passing through the narrow channel spanned by a railroad bridge, it enters Pine Lake. To the east the larger arm of the lake may be plainly seen stretching away southward to Boyne City.

BOYNE CITY is an enterprising little town whose interests are mostly lumber. It does not command the special attention of visitors, although from this point the Boyne River may be reached (see also page 40), where fine trout fishing is to be found.

EAST JORDAN is more often visited by tourists because of the beautiful trip on Pine Lake and also for the unusually fine opportunities for fishing to be found in that region.

The South Arm is hidden for several miles, lying behind a point on the west shore. As we round this point Ironton comes in view, a little town once the basis of operations of the Pine Lake Iron Co., whose ruined and deserted blast furnaces, where iron ore was converted into pig iron, still remain. Beyond is seen a large group of old charcoal kilns which, in the rear view as the steamer leaves the town, look like huge old-fashioned bee hives and add a quaint touch to the landscape.

Immediately upon leaving Ironton the steamer enters the narrows, where an old-fashioned scow ferry may be seen which transports pedestrians and teams from the "pensnsula" to the mainland. The channel at this point becomes very narrow. As we leave the narrows a bay may be noted on the east side, said to be famous bass fishing grounds. Some distance ahead an island comes into view. This is Holy Island, so called because it was used as a place of "worship" by the Mormons in the days of King Strang (1850) of Beaver Island fame. Just why this island was selected is not plain, but there is no question of the fact as a matter of history. The journey now leads through a more or less narrow arm until rounding Lone Point, East Jordan appears to the east and the landing is quickly made. The little steamer usually makes several landings en route. These stops at the little docks and settlements contribute an added interest to a most delightful trip.

Jordan River and Deer Creek, both close to the village of East Jordan, are among the finest trout streams in northern Michigan. They are streams of great beauty and considerable size, and they have long been famous among the disciples of Isaac Walton. A conveyance should be taken from East Jordan to points from four to eight miles up the streams, which may then be fished down as far as desired, where the teams will be in waiting for the return to town. Ordinarily from three to four miles is a big day's work in fishing a trout stream. Certainly it is all that can be properly fished under ordinary circumstances. If desired, these streams can be fished in a boat (taken by wagon from East Jordan), a skilled oarsman being required, however, as the current is swift. Wading boots are very desirable, but not absolutely necessary.

Monroe Creek is a small stream which empties into South Arm directly across the bay from East Jordan. Less ambitious anglers will find this a pleasant and accessible trout stream. "Still fishing" is reasonably successful along the banks of the bay.

2 Charlevoix to East Jordan by carriage road.

The trip from Charlevoix to East Jordan may be made very pleasantly by carriage or bicycle. The roads are by no means perfect; some hill climbing will be encountered, but no formidable difficulties present themselves, and on the whole the roads are very good and enjoyable. The trip may be taken down one side of the arm and up the other—the roads are about equally good and this will add a variety to the tour. A pleasant combination tour for bicyclers is to go to East Jordan by wheel and return by steamer, or vice versa. Although a little better road may be had by keeping above Ironton, the gain is very slight and the tourist is strongly recommended to visit this little town. The old iron furnace and charcoal kiln will be full of interest.

Leaving Charlevoix, then, the route lies past the Bellvedere hotel and then parallel with the railroad track for a short distance. The large building on the shore is the D. M. Ferry Seed Co's warehouse, where fine seeds, especially peas of which this region produces a superior quality, are stored. A little further on the road crosses the railroad track, and ascending a little way a small hill, we keep to the left road and follow parallel with the track, now on the right hand, to a short but steep hill. Climbing this we find sand for a short distance, and just here a sandy road (there is promise that it may be graveled this season) continues to the left across a rough stretch of country. This road may be followed to Ironton if desired, and after a mile and a half of sand it becomes hard and good, and affords many pretty vistas of the lake.

But we will describe the other route, in which we keep to the right, and after a gentle descent (good road) we climb a long but easy grade, well graveled, to a little white school house (3 miles from Charlevoix) with a log house immediately beyond. The road leads straight on to the head of a small lake called Newman's Lake, where it deflects to the left a little, and then immediately we turn to the right again and climb a steep hill to find the lake close at our right. From this point we follow to the foot of a short, steep hill. This hill we do not climb, but turning to the left, follow straight on, avoiding the road to the right, to where the road crosses another at right angles; we keep straight ahead up a series of hills which look more formidable in the distance than they really are. Reaching the crest of the hill, we come in a little time to a four corners. This is the place where the other road mentioned above joins our road.

Our journey takes us straight on for a mile, where Ironton appears in view, and descending the hill with the little town on the left, we reach the quaint old ferry. This ferry is operated at county expense, therefore no charge is made for transportation. Doubtless the old ferryman will take you over in a little skiff, as the scow is used mostly for teams. After crossing the arm, we proceed on the journey through the peninsula. The road runs due east for about two miles, then on passing a schoolhouse on the north side of the road, we take the first turn to the right, and climbing a long, steep hill, reach its crest where fine views are to be enjoyed in every direction. From this point the road runs along the island parallel to the bay. Avoid roads turning to the right. The distance from the ferry to East Jordan is nine miles. About four miles from East Jordan a beautiful brook of spring water is crossed. Beyond this the road is very good to the town. No special description of the road on the other side of South Arm is needed, as the simple direction "follow the telephone line" is all that is necessary.

3 Beaver Island.

One of the most interesting places to visit in this region is Beaver Island, situated thirty-five miles almost due north of Charlevoix. Mail steamer leaves Charlevoix on Tuesday, Thursday and Saturday of each week, fare for the round trip $2.00. No stops are made between Charlevoix and St. James, the single village on the island. The course lies close to the eastern shore of the island its entire length. Most tourists will not wish to remain longer than the few hours that the steamer stays there. To those who desire absolute quiet and rest in novel and quiet surroundings, a longer visit is strongly recommended. The accommodations at Mrs. Gibson's are of the very best, especially famous for her cooking of fish. There is much of scenic beauty, romantic history and novel surroundings to make a visit of some days most restful and pleasant.

The town of St. James is situated in a beautiful bay protected from storms by a long point upon which is placed a lighthouse and life-saving station. The larger part of the village is directly across the bay from the point. The principal business is fishing. Those to whom this industry is new will be interested in watching its operations. A trip in the fish tug will be enjoyed by those whose stomachs are not "finniky!"

The historic interest of the Beaver Island centers in the story of James Jesse Strang. This strange character was born in 1813 and was actively identified with the Mormon church in the earlier period of its career. After the death of Joseph Smith a large number of his immediate Mormon neighbors were convinced of the truth of Strang's claim to be the successor of Smith and migrated with him to Beaver Island about 1849. Strang was publicly crowned King of the Island in 1850. From that time until the day of his death he ruled his kingdom with a high hand. He instituted polygamy, having himself at least five wives. He established an order of "Destroying Angels" who in secret wreaked his vengeance on all who disobeyed his will. He carried on a series of depredations upon the "gentle" fishmen that attained the proportions of a real piracy, and he manipulated the politics at the island in such a way as to escape all punishment of his crimes, even securing his own election to the state legislature for the two terms of 1853-55.

Such a course could have but one issue. There arose about this man an increasing number of bitter enemies, who only bided their time to inflict revenge upon him. Among these was Dr. McCulloh, a prominent Mormon whose house (see illustration page 91) was a center of Mormon interest and who was at one time a confidential advisor of Strang himself. Another was Tom Bedford, who, though nominally a Mormon, did not sympathize with Strang and refused to be party to his piracies, and who had been flogged at the whipping post by the Destroying Angel for insubordination. These two men determined on Strang's assassination.

Early in 1856 the government boat "Michigan" came into St. James to investigate into the disorders pertaining thereto. The commander sent for Strang. On his way to the boat he was fired upon by Bedford and McCulloh who had hidden themselves in some nearby wood pile. Strang died of his wounds some weeks after, being removed to his old home in Voree. Bedford and McCulloh fled to the "Michigan" for protection and were taken with their families to Mackinac, where they were received as heroes. A few months later the Mormons, now without a leader, were driven forcibly from the island without being allowed to take more of their possessions than the clothes they had on.

There is one main street in St. James which leads from the woods on the south, where are the charred ruins of Strang's castle, to the lighthouse point. Just beyond Mrs. Gibson's is the old McCulloh home, the

only relic of the Mormon days now left, unless it be the pine tree behind Mr. Neal Gallagher's store which is said to be Strang's famous whipping post.

Beaver Island is about eighteen miles long and eight miles wide. It is covered with most beautiful forestry of pine, balsam, spruce and fir. Its miles and miles of heath hard enough for a bicycle or carriage, afford opportunity for many charming vistas and superb views. One of the grandest views in Northern Michigan can be obtained from the summit of Mount Pisgah, a great sand dune rising fully 250 feet on the western coast of the island, a pleasant walk from St. James. There are several small lakes on the island whose almost virgin waters offer splendid fishing to those enterprising enough to reach them.

About a mile from the town, south on the "King's Highway" is the little Catholic Church, presided over for thirty years by Father Gallagher, whose name is a household word far and wide.

3. Petoskey and Immediate Environs.

(1) HISTORY— Petoskey, one of the chief cities of Northern Michigan, is charmingly situated near the eastern extremity of Little Traverse Bay, with about 4500 inhabitants normal population. It is the center of business and resort interests for quite an extended territory. Petoskey was incorporated as a village in 1879 and as a city in 1895. From time immemorial its site was a favorite rendezvous for native Indian tribes, and the early history of Petoskey is inseparably connected with Indian traditions. The story of its name is as follows:

CHIEF PETOSKEY.

In 1787 one Nee-i-too-shing, a chief of the Chippewa tribe, had born to him at sunrise, in his wigwam on the banks of the Manistee River, a son, whom he named Pe-to-se-ga, meaning "the rising sun." This chieftan moved northward with his family and in time took up his abode on Little Traverse Bay near Harbor Springs. Here was the boyhood home of Pe-to-se-ga, and when he was twenty-two years old he married and settled here in a home of his own. Many years later, owing to religious differences between himself and the Catholic priests to whose domination he declined to submit, he moved to the other side of the bay and took up his abode on the ground now occupied by the city which was called after him, Petoskey being an unhappy corruption of Pe-to-se-ga.

Previous to this, for many years Little Traverse Bay had been the center of Catholic missionary operations. More than two hundred years ago Father Marquette was wont to visit here with his companions, and the Marquette trail leading between Grand Traverse Bay and Mackinac Island via Charlevoix and Petoskey, is still extant, a portion of which, running through the park of the Arlington Hotel, may be readily visited and is an interesting and historic memorial of these stirring times.

In 1852 Mr. Andrew Porter, still living and an honored citizen of Petoskey, came in the interests of the Government Protestant school, and located here on what is now the Jarman farm, situated on a beautiful knoll immediately south of the Charlevoix road and about three-quarters of a mile from the Mitchell street bridge. Here he established an industrial training school for the instruction of the Indians in the simple elementary branches and in agricultural pursuits.

At midnight December 31st, 1874, the first train entered Petoskey, then a mere hamlet, and for several years this place was the terminus of the Grand Rapids & Indiana Railroad. In 1882 the road was completed to

GRAND RAPIDS AND INDIANA RAILROAD STATION AND PARK, PETOSKEY.

Mackinaw City. The remaining history of Petoskey is that which is characteristic of the growth of all western cities—the advance of all civic conditions with rapid strides. In 1882 it had a population of 2700 souls. In 1894 this was increased to 3649. The growth, though rapid, was wholesome and healthy. Petoskey has never been a "boom" town and has always been singularly free from the evils incident to a place of summer resort.

(2) ITINERARY—Starting from the Grand Rapids & Indiana depot the pedestrian will follow the broad walk through a pretty park, a few hundred feet to Lake street. On the left, across the railroad track, are the Occidental and Cushman hotels. Turning west, to the right one block, to Howard street, the center of the business portion of the city is reached; hence west along Lake street to (one block) Chicago & West Michigan Railway station with beautiful park, approached either by drive or staircase, the latter somewhat long and steep. A little further on a low bridge crossing Bear Creek near where it empties into Lake Michigan, (on the right side, city water works) crossing the bridge we find a winding path along the river bank, which leads to the high bridge above. From this bridge (Mitchell street) a fine view of the lake and bay and the picturesque banks of Bear Creek is secured.

Continuing up Mitchell street (east) the railroad is crossed (two blocks), and farther (one block) the handsome Methodist Episcopal and Presbyterian churches on the north side and Episcopal church on the south, are passed. Continuing up the hill, a somewhat fatiguing walk, (five to ten minutes), and at its crest turning north on Summit street to the edge of the bluff, (red brick house on the left), a superb view is had of the whole bay. Below and to the left lies the city, while to the right the shore sweeps in a beautiful curve. Bay View is hidden by an intervening hill, but beyond around the farthest bend of the bay the large white hotel on the heights marks Roaring Brook; the cottages farther along the shore, Wequetonsing, and a little further the houses and church spires of Harbor Springs may be distinctly seen, while the red brick lighthouse will serve as a landmark for Harbor Point. The farthest point of land beyond is known as "Nine Mile Point," beyond which lie Middle and Cross Villages. On clear days the outlines of Beaver Island may be distinctly descried directly beyond "Nine Mile Point" and thirty-five miles away. The opposite shore, view finest when the surf is running, stretches in unbroken sweep to Charlevoix (19 miles) with the pretty village of Bay Shore seven miles distant. Returning descent may be made down Lake street with its pretty residences to the center of the city.

If a more extended tour is desired it might be advisable to secure a conveyance. Fine views may be had from any of the hills which surround Petoskey. A pleasant five mile drive may be enjoyed by crossing, westward, the Mitchell street bridge and following the main-traveled highway, known as the Charlevoix road, which immediately beyond the bridge makes several turns at short intervals; passing the Catholic cemetery (north side) with its grewsome crucifix, we reach the Fair Grounds, where the road turns sharply and follows closely the edge of a high and picturesque bluff with

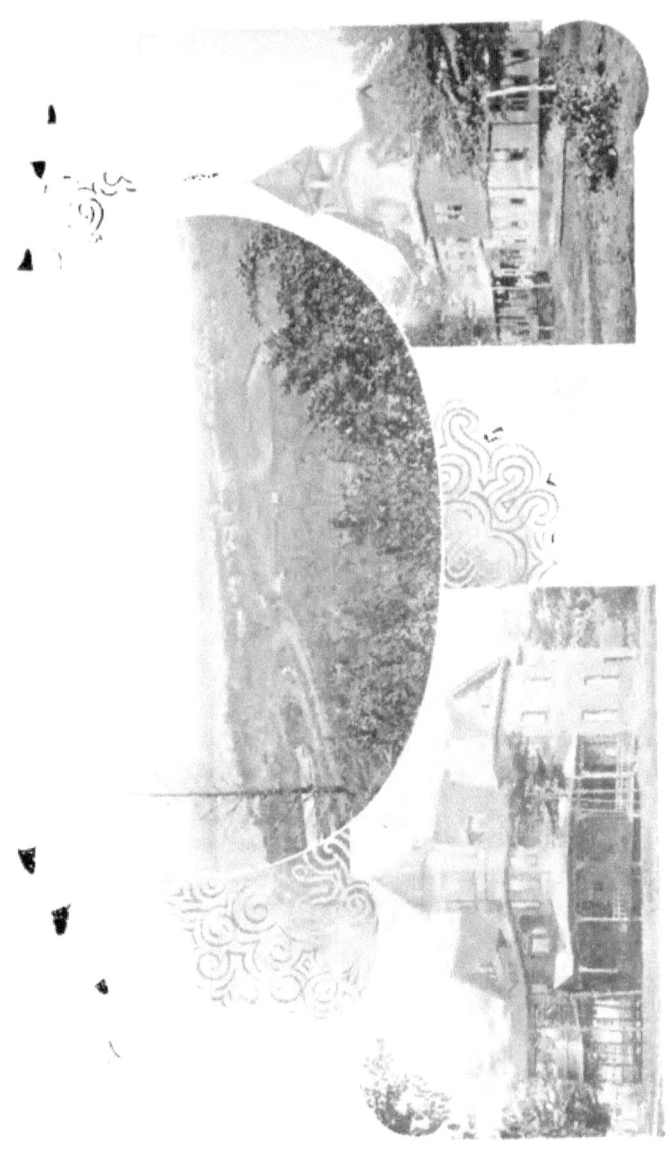

EVELYN HALL. RECREATION PARK AND BAY VIEW. LAUD-HALL.

charming views. A short distance farther on, immediately behind the Fair Grounds, a road will be noted leading to the left from Charlevoix road. This may be taken to the top of the hill, where a schoolhouse will be seen at the four corners. Turning here to the left and passing in front of the school house, the drive may be delightfully continued along the beautiful highlands overlooking the bay all the way, and through a fine fruit farming section. Turning again to the left (half a mile) we reach the summit of Cemetery Hill—protestant cemetery to the left. Here, perhaps, the finest view of Petoskey and the sweep of the bay is secured and is well worth all the time and effort. Descending the hill, we reach the Charlevoix road again and retrace our way to the right to the city (one and a half miles). Pedestrians will find this a charming morning's walk, and bicyclists can make this trip, with occasional dismounts, with ease and pleasure. This tour may easily be made in a forenoon.

To secure a complete itinerary of the city and its immediate environs, the route to Bay View, a little more than a mile distant, should not be omitted. The road lies directly behind the Grand Rapids & Indiana Railroad depot, passing a little park where may be seen a well-defined section of the Marquette trail, the old Indian pathway between Traverse City and Mackinac (see page 93). The park is a part of the grounds of the large and handsome

New Arlington Hotel. Inspection of this imposing structure should be made and the grand view from its verandas enjoyed.

The road, turning here, passes around the hotel and lies along the high bluffs past the lime quarry, which is full of interest—especially to the scientifically inclined. The quarry may be reached by staircase in front of the Arlington, or from the beach. The quarry cliff is 45 feet high (the average height is 60 feet from the water to the top of the bluff, and reaches in some places to 90 feet), and contains a limestone of very superior quality. This formation belongs to the Palaeozic time and the Hamilton group, which means that it is of very early origin. The lower strata are remarkably even-bedded and do not contain many fossils. The upper strata are rich in fossils of many kinds, the principal being Stromatopora and Favosites; the latter name—Favosites (from "favus" honey-comb) may be applied in general to all that coral formation which is so thickly strewn along this shore, and which is become known as the "Petoskey agate" although it is in no sense an agate. These agates may be gathered along the shore in quantities, but mostly of inferior quality. They can be polished, if desired, at  the various agate works, situated near the dock, where many fine specimens will also be found on sale. This quarry produces 120 barrels of lime per day from each kiln. The yearly output is about 40,000 barrels. There are several other quarries along the southern shore.

Further on are the greenhouses, where choice flowers may be had, the sweet-pea being especially beautiful in this climate. Opposite the greenhouse is Recreation Park, a ball ground. A little farther on the railroad is again crossed and immediately Bay View, with depot to the left is reached.

THE WHEELWAY—In this connection should be mentioned the wheelway which is now under construction between Petoskey and Harbor Springs. Already a part of the "way" is completed and affords a most picturesque and charming ride. Following the Bay View road as already described, past the Bay View depot and straight ahead for about two blocks, a turn is made to the left immediately in front of the Howard House. Then crossing the railroad the "way," by an abrupt, short descent, reaches the shore and turns sharply to the right. Riders should keep their wheels under control and be on the watch for trains, and cyclers approaching from the opposite direction. The "way" then takes its course (not open to teams) close to the shore past Bay View and Kegomic (a large tannery) and along the edge of sand barrens, a wild and picturesque country to Page a bathing station four miles from Petoskey—from which point further construction is being rapidly pushed so as to connect with a similar "way" now being constructed from Harbor Springs and Wequetonsing.

4. Little Traverse Bay from Petoskey to Harbor Springs.

Including Bay View, Roaring Brook and We-que-ton-sing.

Little Traverse Bay is ten miles long, (although the south shore reaches out about twenty miles to Charlevoix), and from three to six miles in width. It makes a broad and beautiful sweep on an almost perfect ellipse from Petoskey to Harbor Springs, a distance of nearly ten miles. The shore rises for the most part in stately terraces from the water-edge and affords a remarkably ideal situation for a summer home. Beautiful villas and resorts already occupy a large part of this shore, and a trip around the bay is a most delightful journey. The trip may be taken by boat, train, carriage or wheel. We describe it as follows:

I **By Boat or Train.**

a. BY BOAT—Two admirable steam ferries, the Hazel and the Adrienne, make regular trips about once an hour (see time card in all hotels and newspapers) every day and evening. In good weather the trip is most enjoyable.

b. BY TRAIN—The Grand Rapids & Indiana Railway has established an admirable suburban service from Petoskey to Harbor Springs with trains every 60 minutes. Passengers occupying the open car should be on their guard against cinders. A description of the route by train will apply equally to the boat.

Leaving Petoskey, the train passes the Arlington Hotel, and traversing the high bluffs beyond, affords beautiful glimpses of the bay. One mile from Petoskey

PLAT OF BAY VIEW.

(for description of intermediate route see page 95) the first stop is made at Rosedale, a pretty summer suburb of Pestoskey and, two minutes later, at Bay View.

BAY VIEW—A charming resort and notable summer school. It is one of the most prominent assemblies in the country, being second only in size and importance to Chautauqua itself.

(1) HISTORY—In 1875 a joint committee of the two Michigan Conferences of the Methodist Episcopal Church was appointed for the purpose of organizing a Michigan Camp Ground Association and this committee was also authorized to choose the location. Bay View was chosen and in August 6, 1876, the first assemblage was held. The growth since that time has been very great. To the original Camp Ground Association which controls the property, has been added the "Assembly" and "Summer School," which conducts a great educational enterprise on lines similar and upon proportions second only to the original and far-famed Chautauqua. For full information address John Hall, Chancellor, Flint, Mich. Mr. Hall's address in the summer season is Bay View.

(2) ITINERARY—Owing to the natural formation in a series of beautiful terraces rising in amphitheater form, and to the winding nature of the streets and avenues of Bay View, it is at first somewhat difficult for the stranger to find his way about. The confusion is heightened by the lack of names of the streets on the houses, as well as by the method of numbering by blocks instead of streets. It is to be hoped that an improvement in this direction will soon be inaugurated. Plats, however, a fac simile of which may be found on

page 102, can be secured at the office of the association, and by this assistance desired locations may be found without much difficulty.

A tour over Bay View may be made in an hour, although many hours can be delightfully spent in this charming spot. Following the sidewalk immediately beyond the depot, we turn, and climb the steep terrace, Encampment Avenue, passing the Bay View Hotel and post office (in rear of hotel), crossing Park Avenue, we follow Encampment Avenue in its circular course across the wide campus, known as Fairview Park. At the further end of this park are situated the Assembly buildings, which form the center of the animated summer life to be enjoyed here. The first building, Loud Hall, contains a large and well-selected library and museum, and numerous well-equipped class rooms. The next building is Music Hall, and, beyond, pretty Evelyn Hall, with its charming veranda and spacious parlors. Rooms on the upper floors of most of these buildings are offered for rent at reasonable rates. Beyond Evelyn Hall is the Auditorium, a large though very plain building, with a seating capacity of 2,000. The acoustic properties are very good. Immediately in front of the Auditorium, and in the center of the park, is the office of the association, near by the Assembly book store, while beyond lies pretty Epworth Hall, with a large chapel and other class rooms.

From this point, if time permits and he so desires, the traveler may trace his way past the Auditorium to Forest Avenue, and up the terraces on the left to the highest terrace, where beautiful views are to be had on every side. If hurried, this trip may well be omitted, and, continuing on past Epworth Hall, he will descend to Woodland Avenue, where handsome summer homes are seen on every side, and via Sunset Street down to the beach, dock and boat house. The beach may be followed a short distance back (toward Petoskey) to steps leading up the first terrace to the depot. Visitors reaching Bay View from the steamer (dock at the foot of Sunset Street) may reverse this route, if desired. Ordinarily, however, they will find it more satisfactory to proceed in the order given here.

Continuing our journey around the bay, the next stop is at Kegomic. Here is located a large tannery. The great stacks of hemlock bark will interest the passing observer. This bark is peeled from the hemlock trees from May to August of each year and is shipped in from all the country round. It is worth about $4.00 per cord. The stacks ordinarily on hand represent from $40,000 to $60,000 in value. At Kegomic the train leaves the main road for the Harbor Springs branch, and following close along the shore, traverses the edge of wild, picturesque sand-barrens. The sand lies in great dunes from twenty to fifty feet in height. It is covered with a growth of scrubby, ragged pine, spruce and other indigenous trees and carpeted with moss, lichens and wintergreen. Here is the home of the trailing arbutus which is found in large quantities in the early spring.

The next stop is Page where simple accommodations for the convenience of bathers have been built by the railroad, and immediately beyond is Mononaqua Beach, a new resort enterprise with a few cottages already built. Rounding the curve of the bay, the train enters the woods, and in a few moments stops at Roaring Brook.

ROARING BROOK. Although the name is a rather amusing misnomer (the brook is the gentlest and quietest of streamlets) the place is one of exquisite beauty. The forest is of almost primeval loveliness in its native wildness. The foot path, a good board sidewalk, winds about through charming vistas, gradually climbing the steep bluff which lies a short distance back from the railroad. This bluff, ninety feet above the water, is crowned by a handsome hotel and affords a magnificent panorama of Petoskey, Bay View, Harbor Springs, the Point, with the whole surrounding country, and far out into the great lake. Returning to the depot, a short walk through beautiful cedar forests leads to the beach and dock where ferryboats stop regularly. The grounds, comprising 120 acres, belong to the Roaring Brook Association. Continuing, the train follows close to the bluff on the right and affords beautiful glimpses of the lake on the left. The woods are mostly birches, one of the most exquisite of trees, and this whole region between the bluff and the shore is full of beautiful cottages. The next stop being Wequetonsing.

WEQUETONSING, a charming spot in its quiet loveliness, is pre-eminently a home resort, no effort being made to attract the itinerant traveler, but every effort being made, on the other hand, to preserve its quiet beauty and homelike character. The well-conducted hotel is quite too small for the accommodation of all who would like to come, and is situated immediately south of the depot near the shore. A walk through Wequetonsing (half an hour) should not be omitted. It is only a short, pleasant walk (about one mile) from here to Harbor Springs, and those desiring may plan to leave the train here. The building on the right beyond the depot is Assembly Hall, used for religious and social purposes. Crossing the track we proceed straight to the lake (south) passing the hotel on the right, and, beyond, on the shore the dock, where steam ferries land regularly every hour or less. The broad avenue which stretches along the shore in either direction is lined with lovely summer homes, and presents an ideal picture of rest and summer recreation. A stroll to the left may be enjoyed if desired, but the route to Harbor Springs lies to the right, where, passing handsome cottages for a mile, we at last reach the outskirts of Harbor Springs.

The good pedestrian who desires to accomplish the most in the least time, (cyclists also), may climb the bluff at this point by a fairly good road but sandy, and then following the edge of the bluff (good road) clear across the whole length of the village to the

schoolhouse, descend by a long, steep grade (good sidewalk) to Harbor Springs at the Kensington Hotel. By this route a magnificent panorama of the bay will be enjoyed all the way. Those who do not care for such ardent exercises may turn to the left on reaching the main street, one block across the railroad track, and following it the length of the village, reach in five minutes the Kensington Hotel.

HARBOR SPRINGS—The dock and depot of Harbor Springs are quite close together and immediately across the track from the Kensington Hotel. Leaving the

BOATING SCENES AT HARBOR POINT.

depot, the road leads past the hotel (one block) to the main street of the village. This may be followed, if desired, to where the road climbs the bluff at the other end of the town, and then, returning along the edge of the bluff, descend by another long hill (good sidewalk) to point of starting (see middle paragraph of page 107). But, to simplify matters, the principal points of interest in Harbor Springs are: first the view from the bluff; second, the Catholic Church; and third, Harbor Point Resort.

(1). *The View from the Bluff* can be readily secured from the road which, leading immediately from the depot, climbs obliquely the hillside at that point. This view is well worth the rather fatiguing ascent. Those who prefer it, and this plan is strongly recommended to ladies and persons not in robust health, may secure pleasant conveyances, at a reasonable rate, always to be found ready at dock, depot or hotel. The view is matchless. To the right sweeps the beautiful bay with its now familiar landmarks. Petoskey gleams conspicuously from its bluff, directly across—about five miles. In the immediate foreground lies the beautiful Point, which is here seen from the finest point of view, with its elegant homes and pretty lighthouse, and the lovely little harbor whose rippling waves are ever dancing in the sun. Immediately below, under the steep cliff, nestles the pretty white village itself, and far beyond, to the right, the great lake stretches out as far as the eye can see. On clear days the Beaver Islands may be readily descried lying thirty-five miles away, a little to the north of west. Returning by the same route, we turn to the right on reaching the main street to visit the Catholic Church and School.

(2) *Catholic Church and School*—The conspicuous

church stands at the head of the street. Some years ago (in 1892) this church was built over a small and more picturesque building. Its quaint decorations, the work of its Indian worshipers, especially the elaborately carved altar, made by the Indian boys, will interest the visitor, as also its services with Indian choir. Visitors are reminded that the place is sacred to those who worship here and will preserve a proper decorum.

The school is open to visitors one day of each week (usually Thursdays) from nine a. m. to five p. m. It is presided over by Father Zepehryn of the Order of St. Francis and Sister Superior Wilfred. The present school was organized in 1884, but it is the outgrowth of a school and mission begun here in 1828 when the enrollment was only thirty-six children. It is known technically as the Parish and School of the Holy Childhood of Jesus and has a teaching force of two fathers, four brothers and four sisters, besides several minor assistants. The school has accommodations for 125 boarders. The enrollment last year was 80 boarders, mostly Indians, and 30 day scholars. The school received from the government last year $108.00 per student for 45 students—a total of a little less than $5000.00. All government appropriations, however, end with this year under a recent act terminating appropriations to sectarian schools. Most of the protestant missions voluntarily relinquished their appropriations some years ago.

Besides elementary school work and religious instruction, the boys are taught carpenter work, printing (an interesting weekly newspaper is printed in the Indian language) and binding, shoe-making, with other useful arts. The girls are taught carpet weaving dress making including boys' clothing, knitting, and all branches of housekeeping. Many articles showing the work of the children are on exhibition. The standard of excellence is most creditable. A visit to this interesting school will be greatly enjoyed.

(3) HARBOR POINT RESORT—Leaving the school, we return to the depot, and on from there to Harbor Point, a little over a mile. Visitors may easily walk this distance, although part of the way is sunny and unattractive. They may also go by steamer if they care to wait to make connections with the boat.

The most comfortable way to make this trip, however, is to secure one of the conveyances and drive. Very reasonable rates may be made for a drive through the grounds.

Harbor Point is one of the most beautiful and elegant of Michigan summer resorts. Its unique position upon a long, graceful point of land which, extending out into the bay, gives on one side a fine sea exposure, while securing on the other beautiful and perfectly protected harbor with ideal boating facilities. The outer shore is a series of sand dunes and terraces from ten to thirty feet in height, with a beautiful white sandy beach, affording fine sites for buildings. Behind the bluff the point itself is level, gently sloping to the harbor and covered with a dense forest of noble trees. This forest has been preserved in its natural state and is a spot of quiet loveliness that cannot fail to fascinate all who enter it. The well-kept sawdust road leads in winding fashion to the elegant Club House or hotel, which should be inspected as it is a model of taste and beauty. Beyond the hotel on the left lies the dock—where the ferry-boats touch regularly—and  the walk lies past beautiful summer homes to the tip of the Point where is situated the lighthouse which is open to visitors Thursdays from 9 a. m. to 5 p. m., and is full of interest. This lighthouse is one of the smaller lights being of the fourth order. It has a fixed red light having a magnifying lens of 240°. The government estimate makes its range usefulness cover a distance of 12 miles, but resident fishermen declare that they have seen it plainly as far as 22 miles. From this point the return may be made by either beach. Many delightful strolls will suggest themselves to the visitor, in which he must be guided by the time at his disposal and his individual preferences.

(2 **From Petoskey to Harbor Springs, by Carriage Road.**

Passing immediately behind the Grand Rapids & Indiana depot, the road turns in front of the large New Arlington hotel and follows the bluff to Bay View. For detailed description see page 98. Passing the Bay View depot, the road continues through a long street lined on either side with summer cottages, and turning a little at one-half mile, follows a course parallel with the bay to Kegomic, a large tannery with its row of little red houses. After passing Kegomic the road crosses a small stream, ascends slightly, and then turns sharply to the left (follow the telephone poles) passing a long, narrow pond on the right known as Mud Lake. Those scientifically inclined will note with interest the traces of the Silurian period in the geological formation of the bed and shores of this lake. Crossing the railroad (2 miles) the road now skirts a ridge of sand hills, and passing a summer garden (Moxie's) where another road known as the new Conway road diverges to the right, swerves a very little to the left and continues its nearly straight course, revealing a very beautiful vista of forest-covered hills in the far distance with occasional glimpses of the blue waters of Round Lake to the right and the interesting "Three Sisters" on the left. These are three tall, sugar-loaf sand hills or dunes, a part of a long system of similar hills which intervene between the road and the shore of Little Traverse Bay covered with pretty clusters of the graceful Norway pine. The house on the east side of the road is Mr. Hathaway's. Here boats and fishing tackle may be rented for use on Round Lake. A little beyond, the road descends, crossing a short swamp, and climbs a steep, sandy hill in the midst of which the old road to Conway diverges on the right (4 miles) and after traversing a short stretch of sand and climbing a slight gravel hill, our road turns sharply west (to the left). Here we catch the first glimpses of the bay since leaving Kegomic, and the road follows in view of the bay all the rest of the journey. Half a mile further on the road curves to the right and runs through a beautiful forest of birch

CROSS VILLAGE CONVENT.

and maple, where the telephone line appears again and will serve as an additional guide for the rest of the way—if such guide be necessary. From this point the course is almost due west to Harbor Springs. Near here it will be noticed that the road emerging from the woods crosses through the middle of a large circular clearing. The visitor will be interested to know that this is one of many old Indian clearings, large and small, which may be noted along almost all the roadways of Northern Michigan. Several smaller ones are passed on this road. About two miles further (on the left) a large and handsome farm house will be noted, near which, almost hidden by the trees, stands the Roaring Brook Hotel, well worthy of a visit (see page 105.) Soon the very edge of the bluff is reached with magnificent views, below which lies Wequetonsing described on page 106. To the right a spring of water is passed on the roadside guarded by posts. At this point in the large field on the right are the links of the Wequetonsing Golf Club. A little further and we reach the steep hill descending to the city of Harbor Springs, with its superb view. For Harbor Springs see page 107.

5. Excursion to Cross Village.

INTRODUCTORY NOTE: It is only simple justice to the tourist to inform him that no tour in this region is complete without a visit to the quaint and historic little town of Cross Village. Owing to its isolated position,

Cross Village is little known except in a vague and indefinite way, but this very isolation has been the largest factor in preserving that which gives to Cross Village its peculiar charm and fascination.

One may reach Cross Village in three ways: first, an occasional boat may be found by inquiry at hotels, which is going to Cross Village either on an excursion or to carry freight. No boats make regular stops there. Second, a stage leaves Harbor Springs for Cross Village three times a week carrying mail, fare 50 cts. each way. The mail route traverses the shorter road, which, going through the interior, misses the finest scenery. The third and best way is to hire a team and drive to Cross Village, going by the short mail route and returning by the shore road via Middle Village. This is the route here described in detail. It may be pleasantly made in a day. By following the suggestions offered immediately below, many annoyances can be avoided and the trip much better enjoyed.

SUGGESTIONS: The general rules for driving in this region, pertain with special emphasis here. 1st: the road is much better after a sharp shower, either the day before or during the night. No fear need be entertained of mud, as the soil is such as to at once absorb the water. After a long continued "dry spell" the road will be found heavy and sandy. 2nd: start early—not later than seven or eight o'clock—the earlier the better; first, because the roads are better when dampened with the dew; second, because the air is better for both man and beast; third, because there is no time when Nature is so lovely as in the early morning, not even twilight; and fourth, because by starting early it will give you ample time to wander about the village and give your horses ample time to get rested and refreshed for the return journey. 3rd: take your lunch and take plenty of it. You will have a better one than you can get at Cross Village, with the added enjoyment of a picnic dinner in some charming spot en route. 4th: insist upon good horses. A guide or driver is unnecessary provided some one of the party understands driving reasonably well, but good horses are simply indispensable. By following the route detailed below no trouble will be had in finding the way. Drive gently at first for the journey is long.

This trip can be made by bicycle without difficulty, but riders must expect some hard work. To those going by wheel we recommend the shore road both ways, as the longer distance is more than made up by the more level road. The watchful rider will avail himself of many footpaths over sandy places.

To Cross Village, going by the Mail Route and Returning via Middle Village.

Climbing the steep bluff at Harbor Springs by road immediately above the hotel, we follow the telephone line through the little upper village to the outskirts, where the road turns due north which course it follows for four miles over a hilly, sandy and not very attractive road. At this point it makes a sharp turn to the left (west) and shortly, turns north again, then west and finally north to where, hidden in heavy woods, stands a little white schoolhouse (6 miles). The romantic situation of this schoolhouse appeals strongly to the visitor. The road now leads up a sandy hill leaving the schoolhouse on the left, and through a dense forest whose overarching trees and varied vistas afford many picturesque effects. Later on (8 miles) another school is passed on the right with saw mill nearly opposite. This point is ten miles from Cross Village. A little further on the road deflects to the east. Here the telephone line leaves the road, and passing on the other side of a log shanty, it stretches over the fields and through the woods by a short cut, to join the road some miles further on. The road itself gradually circles eastward and then northward and enters a thick woods with beautiful hills sloping on either side. Then a descent brings us into a sort of swamp with fine groves of hemlock, balsam, spruce and pine. Later a deserted but picturesque old log cabin is passed on the left, of romantic appearance, and soon we join the telephone once more to be a guide for all the future journey. The road deflects to the left in a short distance at a sharp angle (follow telephone) and descending a steep hill, passes a remarkably beautiful maple grove on the right. Then a long, gradual ascent brings us to a point where, straight ahead, the blue water of the lake is seen. With fine glimpses of headlands and the shipping of the straits constantly before us, we reach, two miles, Cross Village.

Cross Village.

1. HISTORY—The history of Cross Village is crowded with romantic interest, being intimately associated with some of the most thrilling incidents of pioneer days. It is one of the oldest sites, being contemporaneous with Mackinac in almost every particular. Before white men reached this country Cross Village was the chief station of a powerful tribe of Indians, the Ottawas, and during pioneer days it was from this place that some of the most important expeditions were formed. Its people were always prominent and powerful in the counsels of the tribes and it was a place of rendezvous and basis of operations second only in

importance to Mackinac itself. The history in detail of these stirring times is given under the description of Mackinac Island, pages 135 to 145, which the reader should consult. We offer here a simple resume of the more important incidents.

(1) Cross Village was originally known as L'Arbre Croche, meaning "crooked tree" because of a large, crooked hemlock tree which towered above the rest of the forest and made a fine landmark for all passing mariners.

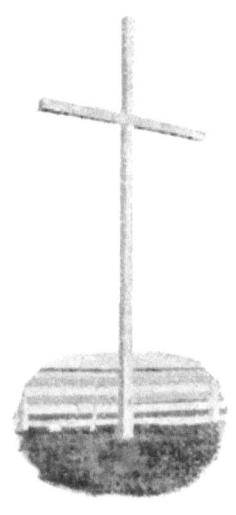

(2) It was the principal village of the Ottawa Indians from time immemorial. These Indians were, at one time, very powerful, numbering in 1670, two hundred and fifty warriors; but the tribe suffered many reverses and after a checkered history, was finally absorbed into the general decay of all the tribes, of which only a melancholy remnant is left. The orignal old Indian settlement was on the beach below the bluff about where the saw mill now stands.

(3) While there is no positive evidence that Marquette ever visited this place, it is hardly credible that during his many voyages back and forth he should have failed to visit so important a station. It is certain that before 1670 a strong Jesuit station was established here, and that from that time it was one of the most important of the missionary operations.

(4) Cross Village was so called because of the huge cross first planted there many years ago. This custom

has been ever since maintained, the Indians regarding it with both civic pride and religious reverence. When one cross rots away a new one is planted to take its place. After the final cession of this region to the United States, no special importance attached to this place and, with most of the surrounding country, its history became insignificant. No records are available down to 1827, when the first cross was planted. The little church now situated immediately behind the cross was built in 1840. Before that time a rude church built of bark was the place of worship. It was situated a few rods south of where the cross stands at the point where so much of the bluff has fallen away. From 1827 to 1855 a succession of estimable priests quietly carried on their work among the natives, eminent among whom were Fathers Barraga and Pierce. At present priests from Harbor Springs have charge of this work, now reduced to very small proportions.

(5) The year 1855 marked a new epoch in the history of Cross Village. At this time Father Weicamp came to Cross Village and there located his now famous convent, farm and school. The history of this remarkable man is worthy of special notice. John B. Weicamp was born in 1818 in Prussia and emigrated to America in 1850. A man of imperious and commanding character, he found the restraint of life in Chicago, where he lived for the first five years, unbearable; while, on the other hand, the freedom and adventure of pioneer life were eminently congenial to him. Coming to this region in 1855, he first located in Harbor Springs, owning the point now known as Harbor Point, but later in the same year he settled permanently in Cross Village. Here he lived for almost forty years, and here he died in 1889: His grave is in the convent grounds and

is described on page 124. Father Weicamp was a man of indomitable energy, imperious character and remarkable personality. To build up such an establishment single-handed in so isolated a location, marks a genius worthy of a better cause. In its prime, this institution, known technically as the "Benevolent, Charitable & Religious Society of St. Francis," owned two thousand acres of land, maintained a working force of forty "brothers" and "sisters"—monks and nuns mostly foreigners—and

operated an immense farm with large herds of stock together with saw mill, grist mill, carpenter and blacksmith shop, machine shop, besides the religious and educational work of the mission. Almost all the articles used were made on the premises.

On the death of Father Weicamp, Father Anton Baumgarten became the Superior, but the institution at once fell to pieces. All available articles were sold at auction and even a large part of the convent was torn down. The farm is now let to private parties.

2. ITINERARY. The town of Cross Village is located on a bluff, about 100 feet high, overlooking Lake Michigan. It has one main street, extending from Wm. Shurtliff's store on the south to that of Orville Shurtliff's on the north, and thence out to the convent. The streets are very narrow, for the most part mere lanes, and the houses quaint in the extreme. The inhabitants are almost entirely Indian and the visitor will find much

that is exceedingly interesting, to note as to their ways of living in a stroll through the village. The Indians as a class are shy and uncommunicative, but ordinary courtesy will usually be reciprocated.

In the center of the main street stands the little Presbyterian Church. Turning to the west from here, we come to the bluff where a magnificent view is to be had. Before us lies the wide expanse of Lake Michigan; to the north the long reef of Wau-go-schance may be clearly seen, ending in a beautiful cluster of small islands. Directly west lie the Beavers, the first one counting from Waugoschance Sound is Hog Island; beyond that, Garden Island; and then directly opposite Cross Village the large Beaver Island proper. Lying out from the dock about eight miles, between Cross Village and Beaver Islands, is the little island or shoal called Isle-Aux-Galet with its large lighthouse. This means "flat rock island" and is pronounced by the natives, Skilly-ga-le'e.

Passing northward, the steps leading to the foot of the bluff, we cross the site of the old bark church long ago destroyed, and come quickly to the great cross. This cross is one of a series of similar crosses which have stood upon this spot since 1827. Immediately behind the cross is the "little church," as it is called in contrast with the larger convent church. This church succeeded the old bark church in 1840 and was the only place of worship for many years. After the establishment of Father Wiecamp's enterprise, however, services here were discontinued for awhile. Later on, Rev. Father Louis Sifferath became disaffected with the work of Father Weicamp, left the convent, and preached to the Indians in the little church. He was a man of great piety and sweetness of character and much beloved. In

1868 he was silenced by the Bishop through the influence of Father Weicamp, ostensibly it is said because he refused to shave his beard; but he remained in Cross Village until 1883, constantly engaged in good works and kindly ministries, perhaps the most valuable of all being his translation of the Bible into the Indian tongue. In 1883 he removed to Kalamazoo and later to Detroit, where he died in 1898.

Just opposite the house, which stands next to the little church, may be seen, leaning against a woodshed, (a little difficult to find) a marble tombstone, marking the grave of Felix Sifferath, a brother to Louis. Felix was also a member of Father Weicamp's convent. He went out one evening to "bring up" the cows and did not return. Search was instituted and he was found a little later hanging to a tree in the woods, having committed suicide. Because he thus died Father Weicamp forbid his interment in consecrated ground, and his brother Louis therefore dug with his own hands this grave and lovingly laid therein the body or his unfortunate brother. In this connection it is proper to say that at least six of the inmates of the convent are known to have lost their reason and became more or less violently insane.

Returning to the main street, we follow it northward to the convent, a distance of less than a mile, passing on the east side the new St. Francis' school, a branch of the Indian school at Harbor Springs. Three sisters have charge of this work, which receives $400.00 annually from the Government. It has about fifty scholars.

As we reach the end of the long, picturesque street, we see directly ahead of us the conspicuous convent. The illustration on page 114 will show its original appearance. The two large wings on either side, one on the east for the women and one on the west for the men, have been torn down, only the church proper remaining.

The convent farm is now rented to Mr. Charles Cetas, who lives in one of the buildings and from whom the key to the church may be obtained. The auditorium is most unique. Its arrangement, whereby each part is separated from every other part, yet all in full view of the altar, gives a most peculiar effect. Passing through the auditorium proper with its low, arched ceiling, we ascend to the altar and looking back see the large gallery above the auditorium where the choir assembled. On the right are the lofts for the monks and on the left for the nuns, the altar with its steep steps being between. Many quaint decorations still adorn the walls, and visitors will wish to linger many moments in this quaint old place.

Passing through the convent grounds, with its numerous buildings on either side, we reach the graveyard, where a conspicuous little square house marks the the grave of Father Weicamp himself. This grave and chapel were prepared by Father Weicamp for many years before his death and adorned with skulls and other somber decorations. Here he was accustomed to repair daily, and descending into his own grave, sit and meditate there for an hour or more. The coffin in which he was buried he had prepared, also, many years before, and he placed it in his cell at the foot of his bed that it might be the last thing he saw at night and the first thing to greet his waking vision. His final interment here was with great pomp and ceremony.

Those who desire to remain longer in Cross Village will find pleasant accommodations. Many interesting drives and strolls abound. The fishing, basket-making and other occupations of the Indians, are all of great interest. Good bass fishing is to be found in this vicinity. Full and reliable information may be secured from Mr. Wm. Shurtliff, the present postmaster.

To Harbor Springs via Middle Village.

We return over the same road (follow telephone) for about a mile and a half to the first road going west. Turning here we follow the angling but well traveled road for six miles until the bluff is reached immediately

THE "LITTLE CHURCH" AND CROSS AT CROSS VILLAGE.

above Middle Village. It is not necessary to descend this bluff, but it is strongly recommended. Descending by a steep grade to the village, a little cluster of Indian huts and shanties, we pass first the unique postoffice of Goodhart, and then, one mile south, we reach the village proper and passing through the main and only street of the village, we drive directly in front of the conspicious white church, and *keeping below the bluff* follow, in many places close to the water's edge, for fully two miles. Here the road is very narrow, the trees almost touching in some places, making a series of most charming vistas. Climbing the bluff by an equally steep ascent, the route now becomes one of exceptional beauty and grandeur. The road winds along the bluff close to the edge for miles, passing en route many exquisite groves, and fine precipitous heights Here a roll-way will be noted where logs are rolled down the bluff into the water and there formed into rafts and towed to the mill. Deflecting to the right, the road crosses a sharp ravine, and returning to the bluff again follows it until within five miles of Harbor Springs. Here the shore stretches out far away into the coast. The road, however, still following the bluff with fine view over the tops of the trees, passes through old Indian clearings with their scrawny orchards and comes at last to Emmet Beach, a new and beautiful resort, from thence following the telephone line to Harbor Springs, our point of departure.

6. Excursions from Petoskey.

1) To Mackinac Island by Rail via Mackinaw City.

The main line of the Grand Rapids and Indiana Railway extends from Petoskey to Mackinaw City, its terminus, a distance of thirty-six miles. Excursion trains are run daily from Petoskey to Mackinac Island via Mackinaw City, giving tourists several hours on the Island. Leaving Petoskey the train passes Bay View and Ke-go-mic (see page 101). Then a little later, on the left, the pretty Round Lake where pleasant facilities for a day's outing may be had. Round Lake is especially commended as a delightful and accessible picnic ground for parties of ladies and children. The next stop is Conway (six miles) a little village situated on the edge of Crooked Lake. Fishing parties often make this their starting point. Beyond Conway the road follows the shores of Crooked Lake three miles to Oden-Oden. This place is favorably known as a summer resort, having two good hotels. Atherton Inn, (now known as Rawdon's, and under new management) is quite unique in its structure. Good bathing is to be enjoyed here; all facilities are provided at the bathing house. One of the chief attractions of Oden is its great flowing or artesian well, close by the depot, furnishing an exhaustless supply of clear cold water from a depth of 200 feet. Oden-Oden is the starting point for steamers of the Inland Route, for which see page 128. Beyond Oden the road follows the lake to the point where it enters Crooked River, and then, with occasional glimpses of the river, to Alanson, a little town on Crooked River where fishing parties are made up for various resorts on Burt Lake.

The road now pushes through a country in which the dense forests are only occasionally relieved by clearings and pioneer farms; passing Brutus, a small village from which Maple River may be reached one and a half miles due east. Maple River is a beautiful forest stream—one of the finest trout fishing streams in Michigan. It can be fished from the bank, although wading is much to be preferred. The stream is of good size, and there is but little "tangle" to annoy. In the early season, May and June, it is best fished from Brutus, but later Pellston furnishes better opportunities as it is farther up stream.

From Brutus it is six miles to Pellston, a small hamlet, but headquarters for trout fishing on Maple River. Five miles east of Pellston—stage meets every train—lies Douglas Lake, an exceptionally beautiful body of water and famous for fishing (bass and pickerel). "Bryant's" is a pleasant fishing Inn on the shore of this lake with daily stage connections with Pellston. A telephone line is also in course of construction.

The next station is Levering, a small village and beyond that Carp Lake, a pretty sheet of water affording good fishing. From this point the road traverses a dense forest almost entirely uninhabited, to Mackinaw City, the terminus. For Mackinaw City see page 152. For Mackinac Island see page 145.

(2) **To Mackinac Island by Steamers of the Inland Route.**

The Inland Route furnishes one of the most interesting and beautiful trips. It traverses a long chain of lakes and rivers from Petoskey (train to Oden) to Cheboygan and affords a constant succession of unique landscapes.

The trip naturally divides itself into three sections. (*a*) From Petoskey to Topinabee, (*b*) from Topinabee to Cheboygan, (*c*) from Cheboygan to Mackinac Island, any or all of which may be taken as desired.

(*a*) From Petoskey to Topinabee, leaving Petoskey by the Grand Rapids & Indiana Railway, on morning train, we arrive (nine miles) at Oden, (see page 127) from which place the steamers start upon the Inland Route proper. The course lies to the head of Crooked River, a distance of two miles from Crooked Lake. Entering Crooked River the experience of its unique navigation will be greatly enjoyed. It is six miles long and very crooked, and passing through dense forests and marshes, presents many striking vistas. The course bends and twists, now among tall reeds and grasses, now under drooping trees whose branches often touch the deck of the steamer and whose outlines are mirrored with almost startling distinctness in the quiet water of the river.

At Alanson, see page 127, a unique draw bridge is passed, and beyond there opens up about three quarters of a mile of straight channel, this part of the river having been dredged out by the State some years ago. As if to make up for so long a straight stretch, the river now bends and turns in angles seemingly beyond navigation, the most marked of which are called Devil's Elbow, and Horse Shoe Bend. The little steamers, however, by twisting, turning, backing up and going forward, make all the turns with remarkable skill, and after passing a typical homesteader's shanty (every one with a camera takes a snap) the mouth of Crooked River is reached and we enter beautiful Burt Lake.

Our course now lies across the lower end of the lake to the head of Indian River, a distance of seven miles. Burt Lake is nearly ten miles long and averages four miles wide. Its shore is quite well settled. Immediately to the north of Crooked River is a considerable point of land where is located the quaint Indian Village, a settlement entirely of Indians whose principal industry is making baskets. Near by is Burt Springs (Johnson's Camp). Johnson's, Sager's and Voightlander's are the principle fishing Inns of Burt Lake. All furnish good accommodations, with boats, guides, etc. At the lower end of Burt Lake is Pittsburgh Landing, the summer home of the Argonaut Hunting and Fishing Club of Pittsburgh, Pa., with a club house and numerous private cottages.

"NATIVES"

We now enter the beautiful Indian River, a stream nearly seven miles long connecting Burt Lake with Mullet Lake. Passing on the left the Columbus Landing, the little town of Indian River on the Michigan Central R. R., is quickly reached, where the boat stops forty minutes for dinner. Indian River has a population of 200. The Sturgeon and Pigeon Rivers—two famous trout streams—are most easily reached from this point. Leaving Indian River village, an old abandoned bridge trestle is passed and soon Mullet Lake is entered and (two miles) Topinabee, a pretty village on the Michigan Central R. R. is reached, the end of the first section of our trip. Those who desire to may return from this point the same day to Petoskey; those going on will here change steamers.

(b) From Topinabee to Cheboygan the route now lies along the whole length of Mullet Lake, a fine body of water ten miles long and three miles wide with high and finely wooded banks. Good fishing. At the northern extremity Mullet Lake enters into Cheboygan River, where on the left is situated the Cheboygan Club House, "The Windmere." Entering the river the steamer picks its way among logs and booms, past a large tannery and enters the locks with a short fall to the lake level. On the right hand lies perhaps the largest sawdust pile in the world, being the immense accumulation of sawdust from the great McArthur saw mills during the last twenty-five years. Those who desire may leave the boat at the locks and walk in ten minutes to the center of the town, having ample time to join the boat again when it lands at the dock.

Cheboygan is a busy lumber center of 8000 inhabitants. Six great saw mills are now in operation. It has a good harbor and boasts a street car line nearly two miles long. Cheboygan marks the end of the second section of the trip and in fact the end of the "Inland Route" proper.

(c) Cheboygan to Mackinac Island. Close connections are made here for Mackinac Island. Starting from McArthur's dock, the steamer sails slowly out of the river passing saw mills and great piles of lumber with numerous vessels loading at the docks. Hence beyond the pier with small light-house, into Lake Michigan, following the South Channel between the main land and Bois Blanc (pronounced "Bob-low") Island. The course is nearly north to Bois Blanc Island, stopping at Point Aux Pins (pronounced "Point aw Pang").

Bois Blanc Island is about twelve miles long and six miles wide. It is densely wooded with forests of pine, maple and birch. At the southwest extremity Point Aux Pins resort is beautifully located with good hotel and numerous cottages. On the southeast extremity an important life saving station is established. Fine bathing, fishing and hunting are to be enjoyed upon the island. From Point Aux Pins to Mackinac Island is about twelve miles.

3 To Bear Lake.

Bear Lake lies seven miles south of Petoskey on a branch of the Grand Rapids & Indiana Railway, suburban trains making the trip several times a day from Petoskey. The lake is very beautiful and so easily accessible as to make it a delightful excursion, especially for ladies and children. A pleasant little steamer makes the circuit of the lake, connecting with all suburban trains. Bear Lake also affords fine fishing and camping facilities, and has many pleasant resorts and inns.

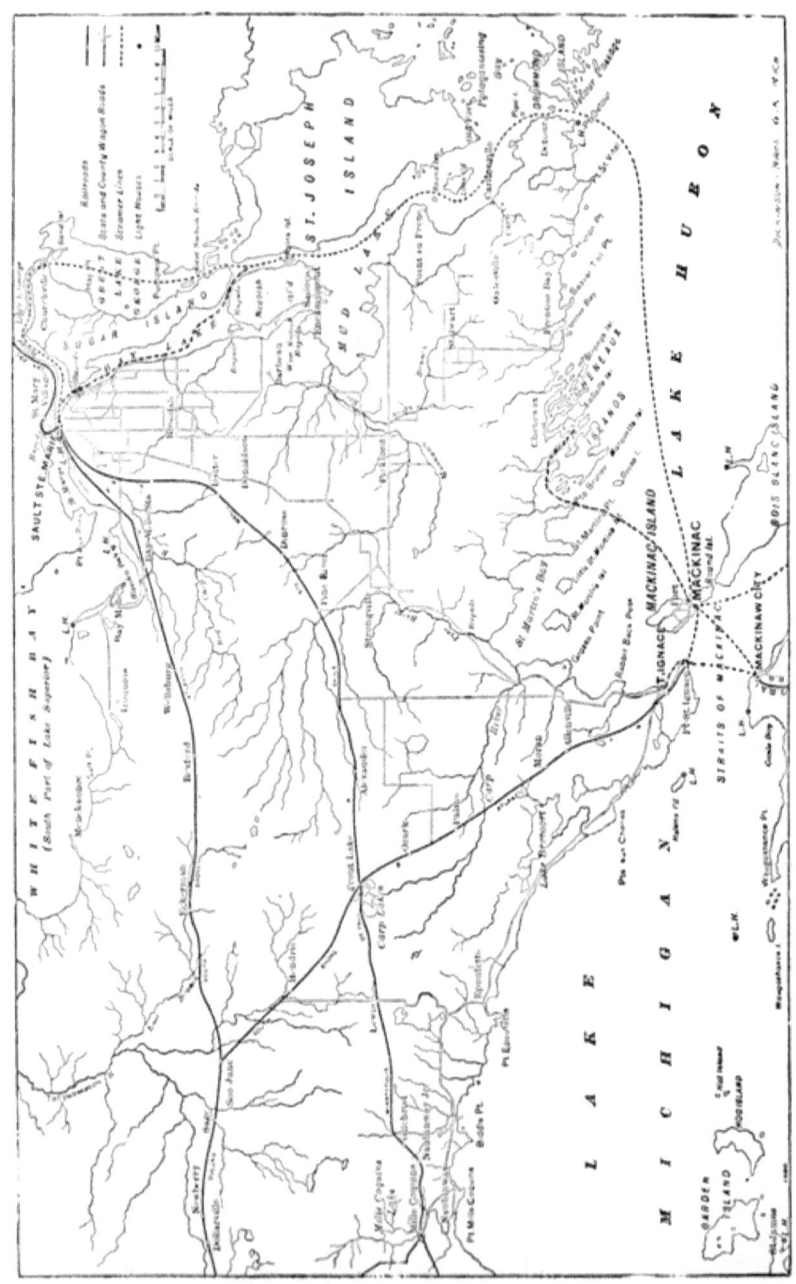

MACKINAC ISLAND AND UPPER PENINSULA.

PART IV.

MACKINAC ISLAND.

(1) **Introduction.**

Mackinac Island is far famed. Its beautiful situation, historic associations, unique and picturesque shores and a certain native beauty that is indescribable, unite to make it one of the most charming spots in America. If there were nothing other than its picturesque situation, Mackinac would be charming, but in addition to this its intimate association with one of the most fascinating and romantic periods of American history, makes every path and height suggestive of historic lore.

In order that the reader may intelligently enjoy his visit to this far-famed spot, it will be necessary to narrate somewhat in detail the history of Mackinac Island. This history is, therefore, presented here in the form of an Introduction so that the itinerary of the Island (pages 145 to 151) need contain only brief resume's of the points of interest, sufficient for those who are in haste, while those who are desirous of informing themselves more in detail, with the historical connections, are referred to the various sections of this Introduction.

(1) Mackinac Island shows evidence of great age and early inhabitants. The most casual observer cannot but recognize the open secret of its geologic peculiarities, namely, that it was at one time completely submerged by floods of waters, whose rushing tides and tumultuous attacks it was able to successfully resist,

until at last the water receded leaving its great arches, rocks, caves and precipices to tell the tale of that mighty struggle.

(2) In the far-distant ages of antiquity it seems probable that this island was inhabited by aboriginal tribes whose very names are now lost. It is certain that it was inhabited long before white men ever reached its shores, and there are traces as well as legends of a history that reaches back into the remotest antiquity.

(3) *Earliest Explorers*—In 1534 Cartier discovered the St. Lawrence River and took possession of all the country in the name of France, but with no adequate conception of its extent or geography. Slowly the process of exploration and settlement was achieved, until in 1608 Quebec, and in 1642 Montreal, became the headquarters of trade and centers of government and colonization. During all this time the Indians came on annual visits to trade with the whites, in great numbers and from far and near. Some came from the Great Lakes, even as far as Lake Superior, and told of the wonders of the country where they lived. In 1633, just one hundred years after Cartier discovered the St. Lawrence, Jean Nicholet made his famous journey from Montreal to Green Bay, and was beyond all question the first white man to see Mi-chil-im-ak-in-ac, now Mackinac Island. Nicholet was followed by Perrot in 1665, and and later by numerous explorers and Couriers D'bois.

(4) *Indian Tribes*—At this time there were two great Indian nations, who were sworn foes and engaged in constant and deadly warfare. These were the Iroquois who lived in New York and the eastern states and who were afterwards allies of the English, and the Algonquins, who lived in Canada and the country of the

Great Lakes and were allies of France. The Algonquins were divided into several large tribes and endless smaller ones, the principal being the Ottawas, Chippewas and Hurons. Although all these tribes were united against their common foe the Iroquois, yet they had constant difficulties between themselves, and many bloody conflicts and dreadful massacres resulted.

(5) *Jesuit Missionaries*—At this time the first real history begins, with the work of the Jesuit missionaries. These men were sent out from France by the Catholic Church to convert the Indians to the Christian faith. They were, for the most part, men of noble character, splendid heroism and great practical intelligence. Gaining from the outset the confidence of the Indians, they became their loved and trusted counselors. They were peacemakers between the tribes, they were interpreters between the Indians and whites, they were intrepid and courageous explorers and opened up vast regions of unknown land, culminating in Marquette's immortal journey to the Mississippi River. It is hardly possible to over-estimate the important part which these missionaries played in shaping and controlling the events of those stirring times. Among the principal missionaries were Fathers Joques and Raymbault who, in 1642, planted the cross at Sault Ste. Marie. Father Allouez who assisted in establishing the mission of St. Ignace and visited Mackinac in 1669, and pre-eminently Father Marquette, whose remarkable history is further narrated on page 154.

(6) *The Period of French Possession*—From 1534 when Cartier discovered the St. Lawrence River to 1760 when the French surrendered Montreal to the British, this whole region, at least in name, owned allegiance to

the French crown. Its history is intimately associated with that of Montreal and early French pioneer life. Being a natural stopping place in the great water-way between the St. Lawrence and the Mississippi, it became a place of importance and prominence to which its natural advantages greatly added. For many years it divided with St. Ignace the attention of the host of explorers, adventurers, traders, soldiers and colonizers who poured from France into the new world.

In 1679 it was visited by the famous "Griffon" expedition under La Salle, that prince of explorers. The Griffon was a ship of about sixty tons burden, built on Lake Erie, near the present site of Buffalo, and the first ship to sail the Great Lakes. Crossing Lake Erie the Griffon entered Detroit River (all that country was then a wilderness), crossed St. Clair Lake, and passing through St. Clair River sailed up Lake Huron. After weathering a furious gale, the ship reached Mackinac in safety, whose beauty enraptured even these hardy explorers. The Griffon went on to Green Bay and was later sent back to Niagara by La Salle, who continued his journey of discovery in small boats. But the Griffon was never heard from afterwards, being, doubtless, foundered in Lake Huron.

In 1695 Cadillac was placed in command of French interests in this region. He determined upon moving the principal post to the Detroit River and did so in 1701. This resulted in a general migration of the Indians to Detroit and the practical abandonment of the settlements at Mackinac and St. Ignace. In 1706 the discouraged missionaries burned their station at St. Ignace and returned to Montreal. But a little later Father Marest renewed the enterprise and in 1714 the French fort was re-established, though in a small way.

It may have been at this time that the fort was removed to the main land upon a site near the present village of Mackinaw City, although that is uncertain. But in this desultory way these settlements were continued until 1760, when the whole country passed forever out of the hands of the French to become a part of the British possessions in America.

(7) *The Period of British Possession*—With the surrender of Montreal in 1760 the Mackinac region became a part of British possessions in America, and so remained until after the Revolutionary war (1795). On gaining possession, the English were peremptory, arrogant and unyielding. They made no effort to win the regard of the Indians, treating them with haughty indifference. This was in great contrast to the genial conduct of the French, who not only continually associated with the Indians, but freely intermarried among them. The result was a succession of encounters between the English and Indians ending often in bloodshed, and daily increasing the enmity between them. The French people, many of whom remained, lost no opportunity to fan these fires of hatred. It was during this time (in 1761) that Alexander Henry, a daring English trader, made his first and thrilling visit to Mackinac and became an eye-witness to the awful massacre at the old fort at Mackinaw City.

In 1763 the Pontiac Conspiracy was formed. It was nothing less than a concerted attack by all the Indians upon all Englishmen. It was to reach from Detroit to the utmost frontier, and its design and execution indicate extraordinary courage and large military genius. Pontiac, a daring chief, full of revenge for wrongs real or imaginary against his tribe, was the originator of the conspiracy. On the 4th of June the massacre occurred. By a preconcerted plan, the Indians, while playing a game of ball (bag-gat-i-way) knocked a ball inside the fort. Captain Etherington and other officers were invited guests, and watching the game, were completely off their guard. The moment the ball entered the fort a signal of attack was given and the massacre occurred. One officer and fifteen men were killed. The others, after many thrilling experiences, made their escape, finally reaching Montreal.

After the massacre the old fort was inhabited only by Indians and occasional traders for several years. Later on a detachment of troops again took possession of this fort which, in 1780, was removed from Mackinaw City to Mackinac Island once more. At this time the old block house now standing, was built, the fort was gradually enlarged and strengthened and the beginnings of a permanent settlement were made.

In 1783 the Northwest Fur Co. (British) was established, to be succeeded later (1811) by the American Fur Co. under John Jacob Astor. After the victory of the United States over Great Britain, this region passed from British possession but was not actually given up by the English until 1795.

(8) *Period of American Possession*—Although as a result of victories gained elsewhere, Mackinac Island came peaceably unto the possession of the United States, it was not destined to remain there without a struggle. In 1783, by the treaty of Paris, Mackinac became a part of the United States, but recognizing its importance and loathe to give it up, by one pretext or another the British retained possession until 1795, when their forces retired to St. Joseph's Island in the Sault Ste. Marie River.

After the American occupation of Fort Mackinac the life of the Island went on much as before, the chief events of interest being the annual arrival and departure of the hunters, traders, Indians and troops. When war was declared in 1812 the British at once undertook to recapture Fort Mackinac. Accordingly, a force of 306 whites and 718 Indians started from the fort at St. Joseph's Island for this purpose. The American forces under command of Lieutenant Porter Hanks amounted to only 57 effective men, and as a massacre by the Indians of men, women and children upon the slightest show of resistance was sure to occur, the fort was surrendered without the firing of a single gun on July 7th, 1812. From this time to 1815 (the close of the war) the Island and fort were once again in the possession of the British. They immediately strengthened the existing fortifications and built upon the high eminence a new redoubt which they called Fort George in honor of the reigning king, but which was later known as Fort Holmes in honor of Lieut. Holmes who fell bravely in the battle of 1814.

In 1814 an attempt was made by the Americans, flushed by the splendid victories of Commodore Perry, to recapture Fort Mackinac. The history of that expedition does not, apparently, reflect great credit upon the military ability or sagacity of the Americans. Starting out July 3d, 1814, with two sloops of war, four schooners and a force of 750 officers and men, instead of attacking Fort Mackinac at once the company was divided. Part went to St. Joseph's Island and destroyed the British fortifications there, part went to Sault Ste. Marie on an unsuccessful expedition for the destruction of British food supplies stored there, and it was not until July 26th that the fleet arrived off Mackinac Island. This delay had given the British ample time to strengthen their fortifications, and especially to arouse and arm their Indian allies. After various ineffective maneuvers it was determined to make a landing upon the site known as the British Landing, and conduct from there a land attack. This was done on the 4th of August, 1814. Meanwhile, the British, having strengthened their position by great earthworks, occupied the fort, filling the woods with Indians. A brave attempt was made by the Americans and valliant fight offered, but under such conditions as to make nothing possible but defeat—this with the loss of the brave and beloved Major Holmes and twelve privates killed, with twelve officers and thirty-nine privates wounded.

After the battle a siege was instituted and a blockade established, and quantities of British supplies were destroyed. But again disaster followed the Americans.

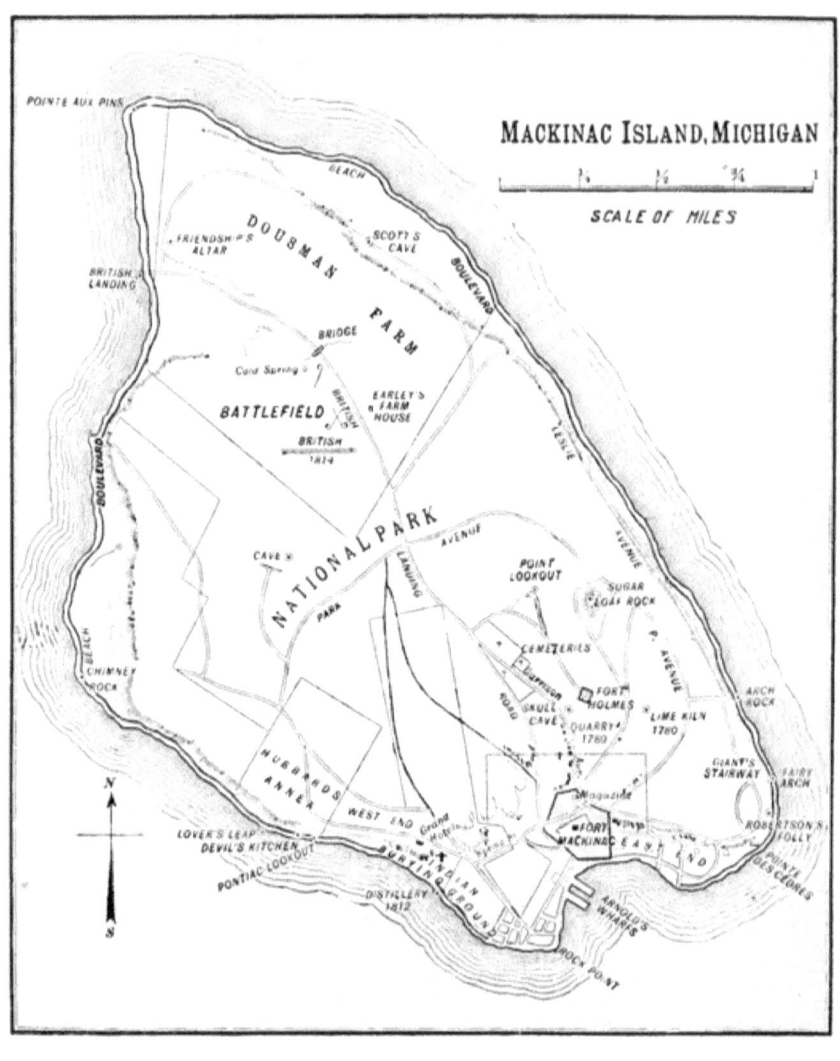

The Tigress and Scorpion, two sloops of war, were both captured by the British and the ill-fated expedition was completely broken up. When in 1815, by the treaty of Ghent, peace was declared, Mackinac was again peaceably returned, to take its place among American possessions. From that time it was continued as a Government post until 1876, when it became a National Park; and later, in 1895, a Michigan state park. Such is, in brief, the romantic history of "the Fairy Island."

2. Mackinac Island.

1. HISTORY—The history of Mackinac Island has been told in detail in the Introduction immediately preceding this chapter. It may be divided into six periods. First, that of aboriginal inhabitants. Second, that of early explorers and missionaries, among whom the most famous were Jean Nicholet 1634, Nicholas Perrot 1665, Father Allouez 1669, Father Dablon 1669, Father Marquette 1671, Father Joliet 1673. Third, period of French possession, from 1534 until 1761, whose famous characters were La Salle, De Tonty, Cadillac and Father Charlevoix. Fourth, period of British possession, from 1761 to 1795, during which time the awful massacre of the Pontiac Conspiracy at old Mackinac, near the present Mackinaw City on the main land, occurred. Fifth, period of American possession, from 1795 to the present time. From 1812 to 1815 the Island was recaptured and held by the British, during which time occurred the engagement on Early's Farm. Sixth, the fort eventually became a national park and later (1895) a state park under the control of a state board appointed by the Governor.

2. ITINERARY—The attractions of Mackinac Island

are numerous, varied and widely scattered. They may be grouped as follows: First, places of scenic interest; second, places of historic interest; third, places of social or resort interest. In visiting the island time is a considerable factor and the method of transportation used. All these conditions unite to make the construction of a single itinerary impossible. We therefore suggest several routes which may be combined to suit the tastes and convenience of the reader.

Route I. The Village and Resorts of Mackinac.

Time, (minimum): For pedestrians, 1½ hours. By carriage or bicycle, ¾ hour.

Leaving the dock, we proceed to the main street (one-half block) and turning to the left, passing stores, bazaars, etc., proceed for one block, hence to the right one block to the John Jacob Astor house; a part of the present hotel constitutes the old fur-trading headquarters of the American Fur Co. This establishment was bought out by John Jacob Astor, then a young man, from the Northwestern Fur Co. (British) in 1811. It was for many years the center of an immense fur trade and the scene of many thrilling and picturesque incidents in pioneer life. Its checkered career closed in 1842.

Continuing our journey southward (to the left) it is a ten minutes walk to the large, beautiful and magnificently located Grand Hotel, from whence splendid views are had on every side. Thence, back of the hotel, along the bluff, are rows of beautiful summer cottages, many of them of costly construction. The journey may be continued to Lover's Leap (about one mile).

Lover's Leap, a large rock of pyramidal form, standing out precipitously from the bluff. Its legend is that the beautiful daughter of an Indian chief fell in love with a young Indian of humble birth. The savage old chief demanded of him some deed of bravery and daring worthy of such a bride. The young man immediately organized an expedition against some enemies of his tribe, and after fighting with great bravery, perished on the field of battle. The maiden pined in sorrow over the death of her lover, and at last leaped to her death from this rock after his death she was wont to sit melancholy and heartbroken.

Descending at this point by a steep staircase to the shore, we reach the beautiful boulevard (which skirts the shore for three miles to British Landing) and return by this boulevard to the town, passing en route the Devil's Kitchen, a peculiar cave-like hole in a great rock made by the action of water, together with other curious rock formations. Thence back to town, a distance of about one mile.

If this route is taken by carriage it will, of course, be necessary to return from Lover's Leap to the Grand Hotel and then proceed along the boulevard to the Devil's Kitchen. Those who are limited for time will find it best to go no farther than Lover's Leap on the boulevard, but returning from that point to town, proceed at once on Route 2.

Route 2. Including the Fort, Sugar Loaf Arched Rock, and Robertson's Folly.

Time, (minimum): For pedestrians, 2 hours.

By carriage or bicycle, 1 hour.

Leaving the dock, we turn up the main street to the right for one block, then climbing the steep bluff we approach Fort Mackinac on the right. A short way up the hill there is a long staircase by which pedestrians may ascend to the old block house. Those who drive will stop at the first gate, and on entering will do well to proceed at once to the old block house, where our itinerary commences.

FORT MACKINAC. The old block house was built in 1780 and is a part of the oldest structure of the Fort (see page 140). Passing along the upper path, we notice to

the left two officer's houses built in 1876, and further on the old flag stand with another group of officers' houses erected in 1835. Descending the steps on the right, we come into the barracks and at once pass a quaint old stone building which was the officers' headquarters in

1780. The wooden building on the right was the hospital, and along the square are located many buildings, both old and new, used for various barrack purposes. Continuing to the left to the corner of the Fort, we come out upon the old parapet where a magnificent view is obtained.

The little island with the lighthouse immediately in front, is Round Island with its old Indian burying ground. Returning to the center of the Fort, we come out by the south sally-port into the parade grounds, now a common and ball ground. Here those driving re-enter their carriages and we continue the journey.

Passing out of the Fort by the old brick powder magazine, we turn a little to the left, and thence turning to the right at almost right-angles (signboard marked "Sugar Loaf") we follow the beautiful road through lovely native forests, keeping to the left to (about one mile) Sugar Loaf rock. This is a huge pyramidal rock towering nearly 140 feet above the ground. It presents a singularly striking appearance, both on account of its size and isolation. It is the result of the action of water and a good illustration of the well-nigh resistless floods which once washed these shores. Continuing around Sugar Loaf rock, the road curves back through beautiful woods about three-fourths of a mile, where we turn to the left almost at right-angles, and soon reach the far-famed Arched Rock.

ARCHED ROCK—This strange and picturesque formation is one of the chief attractions of Mackinac Island. The formation of the arch has evidently been caused by the wearing away of the rock through various denuding forces during long geological periods. At present the columns supporting the arch on the north side are comparatively small and weak, and the strength of the arch itself is so uncertain that the crossing is dangerous and forbidden. The arch stands 149 feet above the level of the lake and presents a most striking and picturesque appearance from any point of view.

ROBERTSON'S FOLLY—Returning to the main road, the journey may be continued at once to the bluff, overlooking the town at Robertson's Folly, a precipitous cliff. It was over this cliff, the legend says, that a young English officer leaped in mad infatuation over a beautiful but phantom maiden.

The return is quickly made, with beautiful views, passing the handsome cottages of East End, to the town.

Route 3. Early's Farm—British Landing.

Time, (minimum): For pedestrians, 3 hours.
By carriage or bicycle, 1½ hours.

While this trip is very interesting and beautiful, it may be omitted by those whose time is limited without any real loss. Its chief interest centers in the historic associations of the battlefield of 1814. Passing out of the old fort by the brick powder magazine, follow the left road, passing, in a short time, the old cemeteries, the catholic on the left, the military and protestant on the right. Just before reaching the cemeteries we pass Skull Cave, a deep hole in the base of a great rock, the place where Alexander Henry, the intrepid British fur trader, lay in hiding for many days after the massacre of Pontiac's conspiracy at old Fort Mackinac, and which he found full of human bones and skulls.

Beyond the cemeteries we cross another road (leading to the Grand Hotel) at right angles, and soon come in sight of the Early Farms. To the left in the clearing is the site of the battlefield. The earthwork ridges are easily noted as we cross them. To the right in the front yard of the first farm house is a pile of stones, and among the stones may be seen many relics of this battle, among them three eighteen-pound cannon balls fired from the British guns. See page 141.

Beyond the battlefield the road sweeps on across the Island to the British Landing, and from there the return journey may be made along the shore by the line boulevard to town.

There are many other points of minor attraction on Mackinac Island. These will naturally come to the attention of the visitor who remains on the Island for

any length of time. To those whose stay is short, however, even their enumeration would be confusing rather than helpful. The routes outlined above are arranged to cover all the chief points of interest in the most feasible way and shortest time. Those who have more time at their disposal can, of course, make these itineraries more leisurely and expand them indefinitely.

3. Nearer Environs of Mackinac.

1. MACKINAC CITY—A little village chiefly important as a railroad terminus. The Grand Rapids & Indiana and Michigan Central R. R. have a union depot here and connect, by means of immense ferry steamers, the St. Ignace and St. Marie, with the Duluth, South Shore & Atlantic Railway at St. Ignace. These boats

are worthy of special notice. They carry a train of sixteen cars at once and are so constructed as to crush their passage through the thickest ice with ease, thus continuing the service without interruption summer and winter. See cut page 156.

Mackinaw City is a small village situated upon the most northerly point of the lower peninsula. Visitors will keep in mind, however, that the railroad dock faces not north, but almost due east. Looking out from the dock the mainland stretches in a pretty bay on the right hand side. Directly in front and distant about eight miles, lies Bois Blanc (pronounced "Bob-low") Island. A little beyond, to the north, lies Mackinac Island with Round Island between. Beyond this an immense round lighthouse will be seen standing in an isolated position upon one of the smaller islands of St. Martin's Bay. While to the left hand, due north, lies St. Ignace and the upper peninsula. If time permits, a stroll through Mackinaw City will be interesting. Crossing the Grand Rapids & Indiana tracks, the visitor should pass the little M. E. Church, and follow westward along the shore to the lighthouse, a distance of about two miles. At this point the narrowest passage of the straits is reached and an imposing view of passing shipage enjoyed. The distance to the opposite shore is four miles. Here, too, is the site of the old Fort Mackinac where the massacre of Pontiac's Conspiracy occured in 1763 (see page 139).

2. ST. IGNACE An interesting city known in native parlance as "Shoestring town" because it consists almost entirely of one long street extending for four miles along the shore. At the most southern point is the old Martell blast furnace for reducing iron ore to pig iron, but not now in operation. Many beautiful drives can be had about St. Ignace, the roads being especially fine.

From St. Ignace to Rabbit's Back, a bold bluff up the shore, north from St. Ignace (4 miles), much of the scenery vies with that of Mackinac Island. And another fine drive is across the point to the Lake Michigan shore and thence west along the shore road indefinitely, passing (at 4 miles) the imposing Eagle's Nest rock which is almost the counterpart and fully the equal of Sugar Loaf on Mackinac Island. The roads about St. Ignace are specially attractive for bicyclers and a few days stay will well repay the visitor.

St. Ignace was settled by the Indians even earlier than Mackinac Island. It was always a favorite rendezvous for Indians and traders, and was the site of the

THE EAGLE'S NEST ROCK, ST. IGNACE.

Jesuit mission begun in 1671. It is especially noteworthy as the home of Father Marquette, and here, years later, his body was borne in state for final burial. The grave of Father Marquette may be found by walking to the far (north) end of town where, on a side street, about half a block to the left, may be seen the modest shaft which marks this great man's resting place, surrounded by a plain white picket fence.

James Marquette was born in Picardy, France, in 1637. He came to St. Ignace in 1668 and founded the St. Ignatius mission. His "Relations"—reports sent to Jesuit headquarters at Paris—form a priceless history of these early times. For four years Marquette conducted this mission, traveling from St. Ignace to Sault Ste. Marie and winning everywhere the love and confidence of all, especially the Indians. In 1672 he received, to his great joy, a commission from the French Government of Canada to accompany Father Joliet on the voyage of discovery to the Mississippi River. He started on the 17th of May, 1673, and paddling in birch-bark canoes across Lake Michigan to the foot of Green Bay, the party entered the Fox River, reached the portage, then traveled across Wisconsin for fifty miles to the Wisconsin River which they followed nearly one hundred miles and reached its mouth, where it enters the Mississippi at a point just below Prairie du Chien on the 17th of June—just one month later. They explored the Mississippi to a point below the mouth of the Arkansas River, a distance of nearly a thousand miles, and returned by way of the Illinois River to Lake Michigan, hence northward to Green Bay again which they reached in September of the same year.

In 1674 Marquette sailed once more to the foot of Lake Michigan (Chicago) and in May, 1675, conscious that his strength was failing fast, he determind to return to his old home at St. Ignace to die. He was able to get only as far as a little stream near Sleeping Bear Point now known as Pierre Marquette River, where he became so feeble that he could travel no more.

Tenderly the Indians lifted him from the canoe and placed him in a hastily prepared wigwam. Here, in a few hours, he died, and here his sorrowing companions buried him. Two years later an imposing array of thirty canoes set forth to that lonely grave and, disinterring the beloved remains, they brought them back in high state to his old home at St. Ignace where, on June 9th, 1677, they were buried in the old mission church. This church was afterwards (1706) burned, but many years later (1877) the foundations of the old church were discovered and beneath them the remains of Marquette. The present monument was erected upon this sacred and historic spot, the site of the old church, July 7th, 1895.

3. LES CHENEAU (familiarly known as "The Snows")— A beautiful group of over one hundred islands lying between Mackinac Island and Detour, fourteen miles from Mackinac Island. Steamers run daily from St. Ignace and the Island to the Snows. A journey through this exquisite archipelago is most beautiful, with its maze of winding channels. Numerous beautiful resorts have been established en route and the fishing is exceptionally fine.

4. From Mackinac Island to Sault Ste. Marie.

By Steamer via the Sault Ste. Marie River.

One of the most interesting and beautiful trips in Northern Michigan. The scenery of the "Soo" River rivals much of the scenery of the Hudson River, while the peculiarities of its navigation afford constant, absorbing, interest. The river is the connecting highway for the enormous shipping of Lake Superior and millions of dollars have been spent by the Government in the perfection and annual maintenance of its navigation. Added to the natural beauty of its shores is the imposing procession of ships of all descriptions that are passed en route.

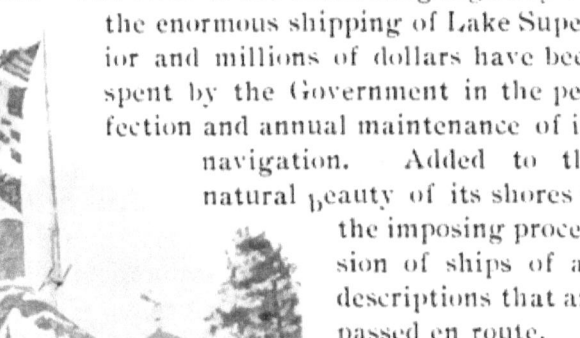

Leaving Mackinac Island, the steamer skirts the southeastern corner of the Island, affording fine views of the village, Robertson's Folly and the whole northeast shore. The course is almost due east (in nautical parlance east one-half north) to Detour, a distance of 40 miles. The little island opposite Mackinac, with its pretty lighthouse, is Round Island an old and favorite rendezvous of the Indians, where is located an interesting old Indian burying ground. The long island, which might easily be mistaken for a part of the mainland to the right, beyond Round Island is Bois Blanc (pronounced "Bob-blow") Island and we follow in sight of its shores for sixteen miles, while away to the left lies the mainland of the upper peninsula with the beautiful archipelago of Les Cheneau Islands ("Snows") between.

After passing the further point of Bois Blanc Island, the great lighthouse of Spectacle Reef appears to the right in the distance. This very dangerous reef is one mile long and three-eights of a mile wide, runing due east and west with an average shoal depth of two feet. The lighthouse is one of the first order and has a white light varied by a red flash. The ship soon rounds Detour Point with its tall white lighthouse, and enters the mouth of the "Soo" river, passing a great iron buoy with large, arched framework above. This is known as a gas buoy. There are four of them in the river. They are charged with illuminating gas sufficient to burn for eight months, the regular navigation season, and have a light which burns continuously day and night. The light is equipped with a perfect and ingenius machinery whereby it becomes a flash-light, burning for ten seconds out of every minute, with an intermission of fifty seconds. As we reach Detour we pass close to a little island known as Frying-pan Island, upon which is built a small range light. The Arnold line of steamers stops at this quaint little town of Detour with its four great docks, but other steamers make no stops on the river.

Approaching Detour the entrance to the river presents an imposing sight. Before us lies a bewildering archipelago of beautiful islands, large and small, whose channels stretch away into the far distance. To the right is the large Drummond's Island, the site of an old Mormon settlement. Immediately ahead is Pipe Island, and beyond that the long and narrow Lime Island, while in the further distance the high hills of St. Joseph's Island (Canada) afford a conspicuous landmark. The numerous other islands are not named.

Leaving Detour, the course leads past Pipe Island, with a lighthouse, and deflects a little westward to round Lime Island, whose bank it closely skirts, passing in time the pretty resort of Lime Island Club (Davenport's). We now pass between Lime Island on the right and a smaller island on the left, and find the highlands of St. Joseph Island dead ahead. St. Joseph's Island is the largest in the river and belongs to Canada. It was to this island that the British troops retreated on the evacuation of Fort Mackinac in 1795, and from this island the British expedition started to recapture Fort Mackinac in 1812.

The steamer follows the coast of St. Joseph's for its entire length, when turning sharply eastward at the southern end of Nebish, it passes into a narrow channel with Sailors' Encampment on the right (so called because here, many years ago, a schooner's crew found themselves ice-bound and were obliged to encamp here for the whole winter).

At this point the channel grows very narrow, and as we round the edge of Nebish Island, an Indian word meaning "maple leaf," a little house may be seen close to the shore with a flag-pole on the point. This is the headquarters of the Government "River-Patrol," consisting of a guard of four men and one officer, detailed by the United States Navy to patrol the river principally to enforce the rule of navigation requiring that boats shall not travel faster than nine miles an hour while in the narrower channels. A heavy fine is imposed upon any vessel disobeying this rule and the guard are constantly, though secretly, on the watch to see that it is not disobeyed. From the flag-pole may be sometimes seen hanging a large white ball, which indicates that a steamer is approaching around the bend in the opposite direction. From this point many and various buoys will be noted, a description of which may be interesting.

The stick buoys are tall spars, those painted red marking the starboard or right side of the channel, those painted black the port or left side. Those with alternate red and black rings indicate good water on either side. Large wooden ranges, diamond shape and painted white, will be noticed on the shores. The gas bouys have already been mentioned. Other lights, ranges, etc. will easily indicate for themselves their use.

Continuing through the narrow channel, the head of St. Joseph's Island is soon reached, around which there swings to the right the Canadian channel from Georgian Bay. Ahead lies the old Sugar Island channel which, up to five years ago, was the regular course of all steamers. Now vessels usually turn to the left and enter the narrow and interesting Hay Lake channel. This lies between Sugar Island and Nebish. It is very narrow and the current is very swift, breaking in several places into rapids. The artificial channel was cut out of the solid rock sixteen feet deep and built up with big dikes on the right, at an expense to the Government of more than three million dollars. It took nearly twelve years to complete the task, and even now dredges will be found at work at the finishing touches. This channel has been in use for five seasons and saves a distance of twelve miles between Detour and Sault Ste. Marie.

Beyond Hay Lake channel the steamer enters the

long, narrow Hay Lake, and following the shores of Sugar Island, a long narrow island lying at the head of the river, it reaches, at the far end, the channel which narrows down to the dimensions of a canal and is very picturesque. Beyond this it broadens out into a considerable lake, and with a sharp turn westward sweeps up to the rapids with a fine approach to the two cities of Sault Ste. Marie, Canadian and American, lying on either side.

WRECK OF THE "MARK HOPKINS" IN HAY LAKE CHANNEL.

THE LOCKS AT SAULE STE. MARIE.

Sault Ste. Marie.

1. HISTORY—The history of Sault Ste. Marie is intimately connected with early Indian pioneer life in this country, a narrative of which will be found in the Introduction of this Part. In addition it may be noted of Sault Ste. Marie that the early fishing and camping grounds were along the rapids. It was first claimed by the French in 1641. In that year a Jesuit mission station was established under Raymbault and Joques. In 1671 occurred a great pageant—a gathering of all tribes and peoples to acknowledge allegience to the King of France. This was done with great pomp and ceremony. The original copy of the Process-Verbal used in this ceremony is found in the Jesuit "Relations" of 1671. We reprint it here as affording a vivid glimpse of these stirring and picturesque pioneer times.

PROCESS VERBAL.

"Simon Francois Dumont, esquire, Sieur de Saint Lusson, commissioned subdelegate of Monseigneur, the Intendant of New France....

"In accordance with the orders we have received from Monseigneur, the Intendant of New France, the 3d of last July....to immediately proceed to the country of the Indian Outaouais, Nez-percez, Illinois, and other nations, discovered and to be discovered, in North America, in the region of Lake Superior or Mer-Douce (Huron), to make there search and discovery of mines of all sorts, especially of copper, ordering us moreover to take possession in the name of the king of all the country, inhabited or not inhabited, through which we may pass....We, in virtue of our commission, have made our first disembarkment at the village or burg of Sainte Marie du Sault, the place where the Rev. Jesuit Fathers make their mission, and where the Indian tribes, called Achipoes, Malamechs, Noguets, and others, make their actual abode. We have convoked there as many other tribes as it was in our power to assemble, and they met there to the number of fourteen tribes, namely the Achipoes, Malamechs, Noguets, Banabeoueks, Makomiteks, Poulteatemis, Oumaloumines, Sassaouacottons, dwelling at the Bay called that of the Puants (Green Bay), and who have taken it upon themselves to make it (treaty) known to their neighbors, who are the Illinois, Mascouttins, Outagamis, and other nations; also the Christinos, Assinipouals, Aumossomiks, Outaouais-Conscottons, Niscaks, Maskwikoukiaks, all of them inhabiting the countries of the North and near the sea, who have charged themselves with making it known to their neighbors, who are believed to be in great numbers dwelling near the shores of the same sea. We have caused this, our said commission, to be read to them in the presence of the Rev. Fathers of the Society of Jesus, and of all the Frenchmen named below, and have had it interpreted by Nicholas Perrot, interpreter of His Majesty in this matter, in order that they may not be able (to claim) to be ignorant of it. Having then caused a cross to be erected to produce there the fruits of Christianity, and near it a cedar pole, to which we have attached the arms of France, saying three times with a loud voice and public proclamation, that IN THE NAME OF THE MOST HIGH, MOST POWERFUL, AND MOST REDOUBTABLE MONARCH, LOUIS XIV. OF NAME, MOST CHRISTIAN KING OF FRANCE AND NAVARRE, we take possession of said place, Sainte Marie du Sault, as also of the Lakes Huron and Superior, the Island of Caientation (Manilouline), and of all other lands, rivers, lakes and streams contiguous to and adjacent here, as well discovered as to be discovered, which are bounded on the one side by the seas of the North and West, and on the other side by the sea of the South, in its whole length or depth, taking up at each of the said three proclamations a sod of earth, crying 'Vive le Roy!' and causing the same to be cried by the whole assembly, as well French as Indians, declaring to the said nations aforesaid and hereafter that from henceforth they were to be proteges (subjects) of His Majesty, subject to obey his laws and follow his customs, promising them all protection and succor on his part against the incursion and invasion of their enemies, declaring to all other potentates, sovereign princes, as well States as Republics, to them or their subjects, that they neither can nor shall seize upon or dwell in any place of this country, unless with the good pleasure of his said most

Christian Majesty, and of him who shall govern the land in his name, under penalty of incurring his hatred and the efforts of his arms. And that none may pretend ignorance of this transaction, we have now attached on the reverse side of the arms of France our Process-Verbal of the taking possession, signed by ourselves and the persons below named, who were all present.

' Done at Sainte Marie du Sault, the 14th day of June, in the the year of grace 1671.

"DAUMONT DE SAINT LUSSON."
(Then follow the signature of the witnesses.)

In 1750 the first fort was built to prevent the Indians of Lake Superior from intercourse with the British settlements of New York and the east. In 1762 the British took peaceable possession of the fort, and only reluctantly relinquished their claim upon it after the Revolutionary War. As late as 1820 Gov. Cass, of Michigan, found a British flag still floating on the American side, and it was against the angry protests of the inhabitants that he pulled it down and replaced it with an American flag.

2. ITINERARY —Sault Ste. Marie, meaning "Falls of St. Marie," and usually called "The Soo," is a pleasant city having, in 1894, a population of 7244. The principal points of interest to the tourist are Fort Brady, the Locks and the Rapids. A stroll through the city and visit to the quaint little Canadian "Soo" across the river (ferryboat once an hour) should, of course, be added.

Fort Brady, situated above the locks on a beautiful eminence about half a mile to the west, is quite extensive in its appointments and will be a point of great interest to the visitor. The ceremony of raising the flag at sunrise and lowering it at sunset will be found of special interest.

The Canal and Locks. This imposing piece of

engineering skill commands more than passing interest. As early as 1838 an appropriation was made by the State of Michigan for a ship canal and work was begun. The General Government, however, interfered, considering the undertaking an infringement upon the rights of the United States. In 1852 an Act was passed appropriating 750,000 acres of land for this enterprise, and in 1853 the work was begun. The locks, two in number,

were constructed 350 feet long, 70 feet wide with a draft of 12 feet. The canal was opened May 21st, 1855, having cost one million dollars. In 1881 a new United States Government lock was completed taking the place of the old state locks, the first of which was built 515 feet long, 80 feet wide, (60 feet at the gates) with a draft of 16 feet, while the second lock, only recently completed, is 800 feet long and 100 feet wide. The total depth of the canal is 43 feet, and the locks have a lift of 18 feet and take eleven minutes to fill or empty. The total cost of this immense structure was more than seven million dollars. The annual tonnage through the Soo canal exceeds that of the Suez canal by nearly two million tons. In 1890 the tonnage passing through this canal was eight and a half millions, the value of its freight being estimated at over one hundred and two million dollars.

The Rapids. The fall from Lake Superior to Lake Huron is twenty feet, the fall of St. Marie's rapids eighteen feet. One of the most exciting experiences to the visitor is to "shoot" these rapids in an Indian canoe. There is not the least danger in this adventure and it affords an experience never to be forgotten. Arrangements for this trip should be made at the hotels. In the rapids the Indians are constantly fishing and it is fascinating to watch them at their work.

ROUND TRIP RATES

FOR SUMMER OF 1898.

Tourist tickets to all Northern Michigan resorts are on sale at all coupon ticket offices, June 1st to September 30th, good returning until October 31st.

Stop off is allowed on these tickets at all points, subject to conditions pertaining on roads issuing tickets.

Rates from principal places are given below. Further information and rates from other points may be had on application to ticket agents. *These rates are approximate and are subject to change.*

Baggage to the extent of one hundred and fifty (150) pounds will be checked free on full fare, and seventy-five (75) pounds on half-fare (children's) tickets.

STATIONS		MACKINAC ISLAND	HARBOR POINT HARBOR SPRINGS WEQUETONSING ROARING BROOK	PETOSKEY BAY VIEW	TRAVERSE CITY
Battle Creek	Mich.	$12 55	$10 40	$10 15	$ 8 35
Buffalo	N. Y.	22 05	21 25	21 00	19 95
Cairo	Ill.	32 25	30 10	29 85	28 05
Chattanooga	Tenn.	34 25	32 25	32 00	31 00
Chicago (all rail)	Ill.	17 25	15 10	14 85	13 05
Chicago via Goodrich line and G'd H'ven	"	15 85	13 70	13 45	11 25
*Chicago (Circle tour)	"	13 05	12 05	12 05	12 05
Cincinnati	Ohio.	20 25	18 25	18 00	17 00
Cleveland	"	18 65	17 25	17 00	15 35
Cleveland via D. & C. and Detroit	"	16 10	15 35	15 10	13 25
Columbus	"	19 35	18 35	18 10	16 25
Dayton	"	19 35	18 25	18 00	16 25
Detroit	Mich.	12 60	11 85	11 60	9 75
Fort Wayne	Ind.	15 75	13 55	13 30	11 50
Grand Rapids	Mich.	10 00	7 90	7 65	5 80
Hannibal	Mo.	28 05	25 90	25 65	23 85
Indianapolis	Ind.	20 25	18 25	18 00	16 15
Jackson	Mich.	12 55	11 60	11 35	9 55
Lansing	"	11 45	9 55	9 30	7 45
Lexington	Ky.	24 25	22 25	22 00	21 00
Louisville	"	24 00	22 00	21 75	20 65
Memphis	Tenn.	38 95	36 80	36 55	34 75
Mobile	Ala.	47 25	45 10	44 85	43 05
Montgomery	"	45 25	43 25	43 00	42 00
New Orleans	La.	50 25	48 10	47 85	46 05
Pittsburg	Pa.	25 55	24 55	24 30	22 45
South Bend	Ind.	14 30	12 15	11 90	10 10
Springfield	Ill.	25 00	23 65	23 40	21 60
Springfield	Ohio.	19 35	18 25	18 00	16 25
St. Louis	Mo.	25 50	24 40	24 15	23 65
Terre Haute	Ind.	20 25	19 50	19 25	18 10
Toledo	Ohio.	14 35	12 95	12 70	11 05
Wheeling	W. Va.	24 35	23 35	23 10	21 25

Omena $1.25 more than Traverse City.

Neahtawanta 40 cents more than Traverse City.

*Via steamship Manitou in one direction, other direction by rail.

HOTELS AND BOARDING HOUSES.

HOTEL AND MANAGER	CAPACITY	RATE PER DAY	RATE PER WEEK
BAY VIEW			
Bay View House................C. W. Childs	150	$2 00	$ 8 00—$14 00
Howard.........................J. W. Howard	100	2 00	7 00— 12 00
Cottages...........................M. V. Brown			on application
Cottages............................J. H. Purvis			on application
Cottages...........................E. F. Meech			on application
Cottages.........................Chas. Powell			on application
Cottages...............................Jos. Nash			on application
Cottages...................Mrs. C. A. Fellows			on application
Cottages.......................Mrs. E. A. Day			on application
Cottages..................Mrs. A. W. Bushee			on application
Cottages.........................Mrs. Compton			on application
Cottages............................Mrs. Frain			on application
Cottages....................Mrs. Milo Lewis			on application
Cottages........................Mrs. Hodgman			on application
BURT LAKE			
Cottages......................Mrs. E. H. Sager			on application
Cottages........................John Johnson			on application
Cottages....................Geo. Voigtlander			7 00—$10 00
BEAR LAKE			
Hotel Mizer........................C. S. Mizer	75	1 50	7 00— 10 00
Cottages........................Jos. McConell			7 00— 10 00
BELLAIRE			
Waldmere...................Williams & Bump	100	1 00 — 1 50	
CHARLEVOIX			
The Inn............................B T. Osborn	400	3 00 — 5 00	14 00 - 28 00
Chicago Resort...................W. Patty	100	2 50	
Belvedere........................R. P. Foley	100		14 00
Fountain City...................J. H Messler	75	2 00	10 00— 14 00
Bartlett.....................Dr. L. B. Bartlett	75	1 50 — 2 50	
Cottages................................C. Y Cook			on application
Cottages......................Wm. M. Miller			on application
Cottages..................Mrs. L. Blanchard			on application
Cottages..................Mrs. Nelson Ainslee			on application
Cottages..................Mrs. O. S. Washburn			on application
Cottages..................Mrs. Harriet West			on application
Cottages................Mrs. Harrison Bedford			on application
Cottages..................Mrs. Fred Smith			on application
Cottages..................Mrs. C. Lamoreaux			on application
Cottages..................Mrs Geo. Eagleton			on application
Cottages..................Mrs. Chas. Newman			on application
Cottages........................W. H. Francis			on application
Cottages........................P. D. Campbell			on application
Cottages......................Mrs. G. O. Scott			on application
CHEBOYGAN.			
Read..............................H. S. Read	70	2 00	
New Cheboygan........................	70	2 00	
Summit............................R. N. Hyde	50	1 00	
EDGEWOOD			
Cottages........................Mrs. Lathrop			on application
Cottages........................Miss Lewis			on application
ELLSWORTH			
Orient...	50	1 50	
ELK RAPIDS			
Lake View.........................T. E. Sharp	75	1 00 — 2 00	4 00 — 10 00

HOTELS AND BOARDING HOUSES.

HOTEL AND MANAGER	CAPACITY	RATE PER DAY	RATE PER WEEK
EMMET BEACH			
Emmet Beach.....................E. I. Ferguson	75	$2 00	$ 8 00 – $10 00
FOUNTAIN POINT			
Fountain Point...............................	70	....	7 50 – 12 00
HARBOR POINT			
Harbor Point Club............................	200	2 50 – $4 00	17 50 – 24 00
HARBOR SPRINGS			
Dewey.........................W. H. Dewey	200	2 50 – 3 00	12 00 – 16 00
Emmet.........................E. I. Ferguson	40	1 00 – 1 50	5 00 – 7 00
INDIAN RIVER			
Alcove.......................................	75	2 00	10 00 – 12 00
LES CHENEAUX ISLANDS			
Islington......................Melbers & Co.	100	2 00 – 2 50	....
Elliott........................A. H. Beach	75	2 00	....
LIME ISLAND			
Lime Island Hotel...........F. O. Davenport	50	2 00	12 00
MACKINAC ISLAND			
Grand..............................J. R. Hayes	700	3 00 – 5 00	....
Jno. Jacob Astor.....................Jno. Bogan	200	2 50 – 3 00	14 00 – 17 50
Island House.........Mrs. R. Van A. Webster	200	2 00 – 3 00	14 00 – 17 50
Mission House.......................Frank Bros	200	3 00	14 00 – 17 00
New Mackinac....................F. R. Emerick	150	2 50 – 3 00	15 00 – 18 00
New Murray......................D Murray	150	2 00 – 3 00	15 00 – 18 00
New Chicago.......................Jno. Hoban	100	2 00 – 2 50	....
Bennett Hall............Mrs. F. M. Bennett	100	2 50 – 3 00	14 00 – 20 00
New Lake View....................C. C. Cable	175	2 50 – 3 00	14 00 – 17 00
Cottages..................... Miss Mary Doud	......	....	on application
Cottages..............Miss Amanda Hoban	......	....	on application
Cottages.................Mrs. S. B. Poole	......	....	on application
Cottages...............Mrs. Belle Gallagher	......	....	on application
Cottages..................Mrs A. E. Davis	......	....	on application
Cottages................Miss Mollie Todd	......	....	on application
Cottages....................Mrs. McNally	......	....	on application
MACKINAW CITY			
Wentworth.......................M. C. R. R. Co	75	2 25	
Stimpson.......................C. C. Parkis	75	1 50	
MARQUETTE			
Hotel Superior..............................	300	2 50 – 3 00	....
New Clifton................................	150	2 00 – 3 00	....
Marquette.................................	150	2 00 – 3 00	....
NEAHTAWANTA			
Neahtawanta.......................S. A. Smith	100	2 00	10 00
NORTHPORT			
Waukazoo......................Robt. Campbell	75	1 50 – 2 00	6 00 – 9 00
OLD MISSION			
Hedden Hall................................	75	1 50	7 00 – 10 00
OMENA			
Leelanaw...................................	175	2 50	10 00 – 14 00
Omena Inn...................Mrs J. A. Breas	150	2 00	8 00 – 10 00
ODEN			
Rawdon's.......................J. D. Rawdon	150	1 50 – 2 00	

HOTELS AND BOARDING HOUSES.

HOTEL AND MANAGER	CAPACITY	RATE PER DAY	RATE PER WEEK
PETOSKEY			
New Arlington .... S H. Peck	700	$3 00 – $5 00	....
Imperial .... C. E. Christiancy, Jr.	300	2 00 – 3 00	$12 00 – $18 00
Cushman .... Cushman & Lewis	200	2 00 – 3 00	....
Occidental .... J. E. Vermilva	100	2 00	10 00 – 14 00
Park .... N. J. Perry	100	1 50	7 00 – 10 00
Oriental .... Hunt & Waite	100	2 00	7 00 – 10 00
National .... Geo. Marshall	100	1 00 – 1 50	7 00 – 10 00
Clifton .... J. A. C. Rowan	75	1 00 – 1 50	7 00 – 10 00
Banghart .... P. D Banghart	75	1 50 – 2 00	7 00 – 10 00
Petrie .... A M. Petrie	50	1 00	5 00 – 7 00
Exchange .... E. L Labadie	50	....	rooms only
Cottages .... W. A. Andrews	....	....	on application
Cottages .... A. S. Moyer	....	....	on application
Cottages .... Mrs S S. Gage	....	....	on application
Cottages .... F. J. W. Stone	....	....	on application
Cottages .... J. P. Benedict	....	....	on application
Cottages .... W. F. Lawton	....	....	on application
Cottages .... Mrs. L J. Ingalls	....	....	on application
Cottages .... Mrs. B F Gates	....	....	on application
Cottages .... Mrs Lydia Nichols	....	....	on application
Cottages .... Mrs. A. A. Beaman	....	....	on application
Cottages .... Frank Wilmarth	....	....	on application
Cottages .... Thos. Chamberlin	....	....	on application
Cottages .... C E. Cushman	....	....	on application
Cottages .... Mrs. Jane McKenzie	....	....	on application
Cottages .... H. H. Van Gorder	....	....	on application
Cottages .... Mrs J. P. Mynard	....	....	on application
Cottages .... Mrs. A. R. Clark	....	....	on application
Cottages .... J S. King	....	....	on application
Cottages .... O J. Belknap	....	....	on application
Cottages .... M D Wingate	....	....	on application
Cotteges .... Geo. Williams	....	....	on application
Cottages .... J. A. Gardner	....	....	on application
Cottages .... Mrs. M. A. Lucas	....	....	on application
POINT AUX PINS			
The Pines	75	2 00	10 00 – 12 00
ROARING BROOK			
The Inn .... R E. Park	150	2 50 – 3 00	14 00 – 21 00
SAULT STE. MARIE			
Iroquis .... Guy D Welton	300	2 50 – 3 50	
New Park	200	2 00 – 3 00	
Arlington	150	2 00	
ST. IGNACE			
The Russell .... W. M. Spice	150	2 00	....
Cottages .... Mrs Tamlyn	....	....	on application
Cottages .... Mrs Grant	....	....	on application
Cottages .... Mrs. C. S. Carr	....	....	on application
Cottages .... Mrs. Sheldon	....	....	on application
TRAVERSE CITY			
Park Place .... W. O. Holden	200	2 00 – 2 50	12 00 – 14 00
Whiting .... E. C. Compton	100	1 50 – 2 00	7 00 – 10 50
TRAVERSE BEACH			
Traverse Beach Hotel	100	2 00	10 00 – 12 00
WEQUETONSING			
Wequetonsing Club	150	2 00	7 00 – 12 00
Cottages .... Mrs. C. H. Eaton	....	....	on application

INDEX.

	PAGE
"Agates," Petoskey,	99
Alanson,	127
Alden,	66
Amusements—Out-door,	19
Ann Arbor R. R.	34
Arched Rock,	149
Archeological "finds,"	38
Baedecker Guides,	5
Baggage,	19
Battle of 1814,	142, 151
Bathing,	20
Bay Shore,	69
Bay View,	71, 103-105
Bear Lake,	132
Beaver Island,	89-92, 122
Bellaire,	67, 74
Belvedere,	69
Bicycling,	20

BICYCLE ROADS—

Beaver Island,	91
Cross Village,	115-125
Charlevoix,	87-89
Elk Rapids,	71
East Jordan,	87-89
Leelanaw Peninsula,	60, 64
Mackinac Island,	20, 146-151
Old Mission,	64-69
Petoskey Wheelway,	100
Petoskey to Harbor Springs,	107-112
St. Ignace,	154
Traverse City,	60
British—in Mackinac,	139
British Landing,	142, 151

INDEX—Continued.

	PAGE
Boarding Houses,	169-170
Boardman Lake;	59
Boardman River,	59
Bois Blanc Island,	132
Boyne City,	85
Boyne Falls,	40
Buoys,	158, 160
Burt Lake,	129
Brutus,	127
Cadillac,	37
Camping,	20-22
Clam Lake,	74
Canal, the "Soo,"	165-6
Carp Lake,	128
Carp Lake (Leelanaw)	63
Charlevoix,	47, 79-84
Cheboygan,	131
Cheboygan River,	131
Central Lake,	68
Chicago,	27
C. & W. M. R. R.	27-32, 41-44, 66-71
Chicago Resort (Charlevoix)	82
Climate,	18
Conway,	127
Convent Cross Village,	123
Conley Hill,	42
Clothing,	18
Crooked River,	129
Cross Village,	115-125
Detroit,	33
Detroit River,	52
D. & C. S. N. Co.,	52
D. G. H. & M. R. R.	34
D. G. R. & W. R. R.	33
Detour,	158
Devil's Kitchen,	147
Driving, Suggestions for	20, 116
Douglas Lake,	128

INDEX—Continued.

	PAGE
Drummond Island,	158
Eagle's Nest Rock,	154
Early's Farm, Mackinac,	150
East Jordan,	85
Elk Lake,	72
Elk Rapids,	66, 72
Ellsworth,	69
Frankfort,	51
French, the—in Mackinac,	137
Ferry—Straits of Mackinac,	152
F. & P. M. R. R.	34
Fishing (see "Trout Streams")	22
Fort Mackinac,	147
Fort Brady ("Soo")	165
Fountain Point,	63
Fuch's Hotel,	63
Fruit "Belts,"	29, 41
Game Laws,	23-4
Grand Rapids,	31-2
G. R. & I. R. R.	32, 35-41, 126-129
Grand Traverse Bay,	57-75
Grand Trunk R. R.	32
Geology of Michigan,	14-16, 99
Geography of Michigan,	11
Gypsum Beds,	31
Hammond,	28
Harbor Springs,	48, 107
Harbor Point,	111
Hay Lake Channel,	160
Hay Lake,	161
HISTORICAL SKETCHES—	
Bay View,	103
Beaver Islands,	89
Charlevoix,	79
Cross Village,	115

INDEX—Continued.

	PAGE
Mackinac Island,	135
Petoskey,	92
Sault Ste. Marie,	163
St. Ignace,	154
Traverse City,	57
Holland,	30
Holy Island,	86
Hotels,	19, 169-70
Howard City,	35
Hunting,	22
Huron Lake,	13
Indians, History of—	See "Historical Sketches"
Indian River,	130
Inland Route,	128-132
Intermediate Lake,	67, 74
Ironton,	85, 88
Jesuit Missions,	137
Jordan River,	86
Kalamazoo,	32
Kalamazoo Resort (Charlevoix)	69, 82
Ke-go-mic,	105
Lakes, the Great	12-14
L. S. & L. M. Transportation Co.	46
Lansing,	33
Leelanaw Peninsula,	60
Leelanaw Point,	52-63
Lee's Point,	61
Leland,	63
Les Cheneau Island,	156
Lime Island,	159
Little Traverse Bay,	48, 69, 79, 96, 101, 109
Locks Sault Ste. Marie,	166
Lover's Leap,	146
Lumber "Belt,"	35-37
Ludington,	50

INDEX—Continued.

	PAGE
Mackinac Island,	135-156
Mackinac Straits,	49, 153
Mackinaw City,	152
Manistee,	51
Manistee River,	38, 43
Manitou Islands,	51
"Manitou" S. S.	46-50

MAPS—
Michigan,	6
Grand Traverse Bay,	56
Little Traverse Bay,	78
Plat of Bay View,	102
Upper Peninsula,	134
Mackinac Island,	144
Marquette, Father	155
Marquette Trail,	93, 98
Massacre, Pontiac's	139, 153

MICHIGAN—
Geology,	14-16
Topography,	16-17, 25-6
Profile of	25
Peninsulas,	12
Michigan Lake,	13
Michigan Central R. R.	44
Middle Village,	125
Mormons, History of	80-89
Mullet Lake,	131
Muskegon River,	36

Ne-ah-ta-wan-ta,	64
Nebish Island,	159
New Buffalo,	29
Nigara Falls,	11
Northern Michigan Line,	47
Northern S. S. Co.	52
"Northland," S. S.	52
"North West" S. S.	52
Northport,	60, 62-3
Norway Hill,	43

INDEX—Continued.

	PAGE
Oden-Oden,	127
Old Mission,	64.66
Omena,	61-62
Page,	105
Plateaus of Michigan,	16, 25-6
Patrol U. S. N.	159
Pellston,	128
Peninsulas of Michigan,	12, 14
Petoskey,	69, 92-100
Petoskey, Steamship	47, 50
Pictured Rocks,	15
Pine Lake,	83, 84
Process-Verbal,	163
Profile of Michigan,	25
Point Aux Pins,	132
Pontiac's Conspiracy,	139
Port Huron,	53
Provemont,	63
"Pudding Stone"	15
Pullman,	28

RAILROADS—

Ann Arbor R. R.	34
C. & W. M. R. R.	
To Grand Rapids,	27-32
To Traverse City,	41-44
To Petoskey and Bay View,	65-71
D. G. H. & M.	34
D. G. R. & W.	33
F. & P. M.	34
G. R. & I.	
To Grand Rapids,	32-33
To Petoskey,	35-41
To Mackinaw City,	126-129
Grand Trunk,	32
Michigan Central,	44
Railroad Rates,	168
Rapids, Sault Ste. Marie,	167

INDEX – Continued.

Roaring Brook,
Robertson's Folly,
Round Island,
Round Lake (Charlevoix)
Round Lake (Pestokey)
Routes to Northern Michigan,

Sailors Encampment,
St. Clair River,
St. Clair Lake,
St. Ignace,
St. James, Beaver Island,
St. Joseph,
St. Joseph Island,
Spectacle Reef,
Sleeping Bear Point,
"Soo" The
"Soo" River,
"Snows" The
Sugar Island,
Sugar Loaf Rock,
Skull Cave,
Superior Lake,
Sutton's Bay,
Straits of Mackinac,
Strang, "King"
Sault Ste Marie,
Sault Ste. Marie River,

STEAMSHIP LINES—(See 46-53).

    Arnold Line,
    D. & C. S. N. Co.
    Inland Route,
    L. M. & L. S. T. Co.
    Northern Michigan Line,
    Northern S. S. Co.

Transportation facilities,
Traverse Beach,
Traverse City,

INDEX—Continued.

	PAGE
Traverse Point,	63
Topinabee,	131
Topography of Michigan,	16-17, 26
Torch Lake,	73
Torch River,	66, 73

TROUT STREAMS—

Bear River,	43
Betsy River,	43
Boardman River,	39, 44
Boyne Falls,	40
Deer Creek,	86
Jordan River,	86
Little Manistee,	42
Maple River,	127
Marquette River,	42
Monroe Creek,	86
Pigeon River,	130
Rapid River,	73
Sturgeon River,	130
Torch River,	66

Tunnel, St. Clair River,	53
Weicamp, Father	120
Welch's,	66, 73
We-que-ton-sing,	106
Williamsburg,	66

The New Arlington,
PETOSKEY, MICH.

THE LARGEST AND FINEST HOTEL IN THE NORTHERN LAKE REGION.

Rebuilt in 1897-98.

PASSENGER ELEVATORS.
ROOM WITH PRIVATE BATH.
ELECTRIC LIGHTS. STEAM HEATED.
BOWLING ALLEYS.

RATES, $3.00 per day and up. Special by the week.

✿✿✿✿✿✿✿✿✿✿✿✿✿✿✿✿✿✿✿✿✿✿✿✿✿✿✿✿✿✿✿✿✿✿✿✿✿✿✿

Address S. H. PECK, Manager.

CHICAGO & West Michigan Ry.

DETROIT, Grand Rapids & Western R.R.

These be Popular Lines

——from——

CHICAGO,
DETROIT,
GRAND RAPIDS,
ST. LOUIS,
CLEVELAND,
and many
other places

—— to the ——

Northern
SUMMER RESORTS.

THROUGH SLEEPING CARS
AND FAST TRAIN SERNICE.

J. K. V. AGNEW,
Gen'l Supt.

GEO. De HAVEN,
Gen'l Passenger Agt.

The Summit House, R. N. HYDE, Proprietor.

FINEST LOCATION IN THE CITY.
REMODELED AND NEWLY FURNISHED.
BATHS, ELECTRIC LIGHTS.

RATES, $1 PER DAY.

NEAR M. C. DEPOT & INLAND ROUTE DOCK.
Baggage Transferred Free.

CHEBOYGAN, MICH.

Park Place Hotel,

W. O. HOLDEN, Manager.

HANNAH & LAY CO., Proprietors.

The Best Tourist Hotel in the North is at Traverse City.

If you want a place for real comfort and rest, try it.

TRAVERSE CITY, MICHIGAN.

GEO. E. SPRANG,

PETOSKEY, MICH.

Insurance Agent,

....Cottage and Hotel Insurance a Specialty.

ROUTE OF THE

Northland Express.

✕

Sleeping Cars from

St. Louis, Louisville, Indianapolis, Cincinnati, Chicago.

✕

RUNS SOLID TO

Wequetonsing and Harbor Springs.

✕

Send to

M. F. Quaintance

Passenger Agent,

PETOSKEY,

for information,

or address **C. L. LOCKWOOD,** Gen'l Pass. Agent, **Grand Rapids, Mich.**

The Hotel Imperial,

THE HUB OF NORTHERN MICHIGAN SUMMER RESORTS. **PETOSKEY, MICHIGAN.**

THE ONLY HOTEL IN THE WORLD BUILT AROUND AN IMPOSING RESIDENCE, WHICH PROVES TO BE ITS MOST PLEASING AND ATTRACTIVE FEATURE.

NOT THE LARGEST BUT BY FAR THE BEST FURNISHED HOTEL IN NORTHERN MICHIGAN

Steam heated throughout and in sixty of the bed rooms, thereby affording a most pleasant location for hay fever sufferers late in August and in September. Electric lights elevator—rooms with private bath—modern in every respect.

C. E. CHRISTIANCY, JR.

Lessee and Manager

The Dewey,

▼▼▼▼▼▼▼▼▼▼▼▼▼▼▼▼▼▼▼▼▼▼▼▼▼▼**HARBOR SPRINGS, MICHIGAN.**

Rates:
$2.00, $2.50 and $3.00 per day.
Special rates to families by the week.

XX The finest flowing well in Northern Michigan is to be found on the Dewey Grounds. XX

On line of G. R. and I. and C. & W. M. Rail Roads and in close proximity to the landings of all Chicago steamers.

Lake Michigan and Lake Superior Transportation Co.

THE FAMOUS LAKE ROUTE
Between Chicago, Charlevoix, Harbor Springs, Petoskey, Bay View and Mackinac Island.

— Three Sailings Each Week. —

The Steel Steamship Manitou,
The Greyhound of the Great Lakes.
Luxurious Service.
Cuisine Extraordinary.

Passenger Steamers each week between CHICAGO, DULUTH and Intermediate Ports.

The Iron and Copper District of **Lake Superior**.

❦❦❦❦

For complete information, pamphlets, rates, etc. apply to any of the Company's Agents, or address

JOS. BEROLZHEIM,
General Passenger Agent.

Rush and North Water Sts.
CHICAGO.

Howard House,
Bay View.

This Popular Hotel

continues to rise in the estimation and pleasure of the many happy guests that come each year.

It is a **Solid Comfort** restful and homelike all around.

Do you want a good bed, clean, airy room and plenty of well-cooked food and delightful service? You will find them all here.

J. W. HOWARD, Prop.

It commands a fine view of the bay, being of near and easy approach to it, and less than ten minutes' walk from the assembly building. Dummy station close by. Carriage and telephone accommodations and every attention for the comfort and pleasure of the guests.

Rates: $2 per day; $6 to $12 per week.

Special rates to families and parties staying the season. Table board $5 per week.

The Russell House

BEST HOTEL IN THE CITY
BEAUTIFUL WATER VIEWS FROM VERANDA

ST. IGNACE, MICH.

W. M. SPICE, Prop.

www.ingramcontent.com/pod-product-compliance
Lightning Source LLC
Chambersburg PA
CBHW032148160426
43197CB00008B/813